CONTENTS

1.1 Time and Change

This book covers the story of castles and cathedrals over more than 450 years. But you must remember that other things happened which affected what happened to castles and cathedrals. If there was a war, new castles might be built or old ones improved. If the country became richer, more money could be spent building castles and cathedrals.

Most of this book is about changes and developments. Historians use these words carefully. A **change** is when something is different because of a new idea or a new way of working. A **development** is when something is different but clearly linked to what happened before. For example, every time people improved the large catapults which threw stones at castle walls, it was a development. When the first cannon were invented to do the same job, it was a change. Neither change nor development are the same as **progress** (things getting better). Sometimes they cause **regress** (things getting worse). Just because someone has a new idea, this does not mean everybody else starts using it at once. Sometimes new ideas take a long time to catch on. Why knock down perfectly good cathedrals just because there is a new way of building them? **Continuity**, or old things and old ideas still being used, is just as important as change.

A SOURCE

1335 Master Richard le Tailor was the master mason. He paid his workmen 3 shillings and 6 pence per week [17 p]. Stone was brought from Gatcliff, Barton and Rancome and the tower above the gate was worked on, a portcullis was installed and a new drawbridge made.

Adapted from papers about Carisbrooke Castle in the Royal Accounts.

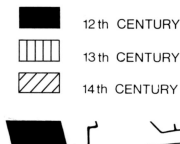

- ■ 12th CENTURY
- ▥ 13th CENTURY
- ▨ 14th CENTURY

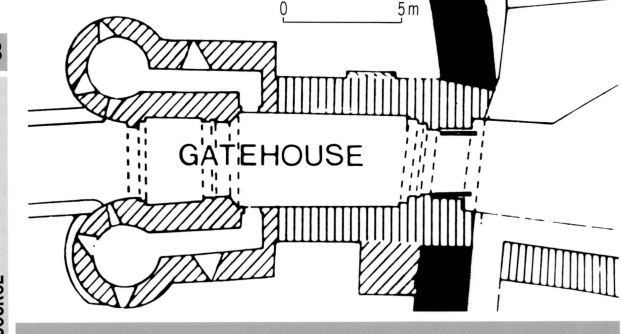

B SOURCE

Part of the plan of Carisbrooke Castle from a modern guidebook.

HEINEMANN HISTORY

CASTLES AND CATHEDRALS

Fiona Reynoldson
Paul Shuter

HEINEMANN
EDUCATIONAL

Heinemann Library,
an imprint of Heinemann Publishers (Oxford) Ltd,
Halley Court, Jordan Hill, Oxford OX2 8EJ

OXFORD LONDON EDINBURGH MADRID
ATHENS BOLOGNA PARIS MELBOURNE
SYDNEY AUCKLAND SINGAPORE TOKYO
IBADAN NAIROBI HARARE GABORONE
PORTSMOUTH NH (USA)

© Fiona Reynoldson and Paul Shuter 1992, 1993

The moral right of the proprietor has been asserted

ISBN 0 431 07335 X (Softback)

First published 1993; this edition 1995

99 98 97 96 95

10 9 8 7 6 5 4 3 2 1

ISBN 0 431 07342 2 (Hardback)

First published 1993

97 96 95 94 93

10 9 8 7 6 5 4 3 2 1

**British Library Cataloguing in Publication Data is available
from the British Library on request.**

Designed by Ron Kamen, Green Door Design Ltd, Basingstoke

Illustrated by Jeff Edwards Douglas Hall Stuart Hughes
Terry Thomas

Printed in China

Acknowledgements

The authors and publisher would like to thank the following
for permission to reproduce photographs:
Aerofilms Ltd: Front cover, 4.3A
John Bethell Photography: p25 top right, p56 lower
Bibliothèque National: 3.2B
The British Library: 1.3B, 3.4C, 4.1A, 4.5A, 4.6A, 4.6D
The Trustees of the British Museum: 4.10B
Cadw: Welsh Historic Monuments, Crown Copyright: p56
top, p59
The Syndics of Cambridge University Library: 4.9B
J Allan Cash Ltd: 3.4A and 3.1B
Peter Chèze-Brown: 3.6A
Committee for Aerial Photography, Cambridge: 3.5B
Dean and Chapter of Salisbury Cathedral: 4.6E
C M Dixon: Back cover, 3.5A, 5.1A
English Heritage: 2.3A, p24, p58 top
Governing Body of Christ Church, Oxford: 1.2A
Sonia Halliday and Laura Lushington: 4.5E, 4.6G and H, 5.2B
Clive Hicks: 1.1C, p58 lower
Michael Holford: 2.1B, 2.2A and C, 2.4B, 2.5A, 4.2A, 5.1B
Musée Condé Chantilly/Giraudon: 4.4
National Monuments Record/Dean and Chapter of York: 4.9A
National Portrait Gallery: 5.2A
Sealand Aerial Photography: 3.1C, 5.3B
Paul Shuter: p25 left, 5.3C
Karen Taylor: 4.8C
The Board of Trinity College, Dublin: 3.6B
Woodmansterne Ltd: 4.2C, 4.8A, 5.2C

We would also like to thank the following for permission to
reproduce copyright material:
A & C Black for Source 2.1A which is taken from *Norman
Castles in Britain* by Derek Renn, John Baker Publishers, 1973;
Cadw: Welsh Historic Monuments, Crown Copyright for
Source 3.4E and the castle plan on p28; Cambridge
University Press for 4.1B and 4.7D which are taken from *Life
in a Medieval Monastery* by Anne Boyd, 1987; English
Heritage for the following castle plans: 1.1B, 3.1A, p25 lower,
p58, p59, 5.3A and C; The Controller, HMSO: for 3.6E, 4.6F
and 4.7C.

Every effort has been made to contact copyright holders of
material reproduced in this book. Any omissions will be
rectified in subsequent printings if notice is given to the
publisher.

Details of Written Sources

In some sources the wording or sentence structure has been
simplified to ensure that the source is accessible.

Anne Boyd, *Life in a Medieval Monastery*, Cambridge
University Press, 1987: 4.7D
Geoffrey Chaucer, *The Canterbury Tales* (Ed. J. Anderson),
Macmillan, 1974: 4.10A
Dean and Chapter of Winchester, *The Medieval Chantries of
Winchester*, 1977: 4.5C
R. C. Finucane, *Miracles and Pilgrims*, J. M. Dent and Sons
Ltd, 1977: 4.10D, 4.10E
John Fitchen, *The Construction of Gothic Cathedrals*,
University of Chicago Press, 1981: 4.6A
J. A. Giles (Trans.), *Roger of Wendover's Flowers of History*,
London, 1848: 3.2A
History of the King's Works, vol. i and ii, HMSO, 1977: 2.4C,
4.6F, 4.7C
Paul Johnson, *The National Trust Book of British Castles*, 1978:
3.6C and D
A. C. Laishley, *The Stained Glass of York*, W. and A. L.
Oldfield, 1971: 4.6I
William Langland, *Piers Plowman*, (Ed. A. V. C. Schmidt),
Dent, 1978: 4.8B
Nicholas Orme, *Exeter Cathedral as it was 1050-1550*, Devon
Books, 1986: 4.5D
Lorna Sass, *To the King's Taste*, John Murray, 1976: 3.4D
Dr Denis Smith, *The Gothic Cathedral*, video produced by
Imperial College/Sussex Video Ltd, 1986: 4.6B
R. W. Southern, *History of the Church*, Penguin, 1970: 4.5B
The Anglo-Saxon Chronicle (Trans. G. N. Garmonsway), J. M
Dent and Sons Ltd, 1953: 2.5B and C
Philip Warner, *The Medieval Cathedral*, Arthur Baker Ltd,
1971: 1.2B, 2.2B
Percy Watson, *Building the Medieval Cathedrals*, Cambridge
University Press, 1976: 4.7B

C

SOURCE

Part of the gatehouse of Carisbrooke Castle.

One of the things historians do when they are working with hundreds of years is to divide them up into bits. English history is often divided into periods according to the families of kings. The 450 years covered by this book can be divided into the Norman, Angevin, Plantagenet, Lancastrian, Yorkist and Tudor periods.

The story of castles and cathedrals can be divided up like this, too. They are divided up by the styles in which they were built. For castles the styles are: Motte and Bailey, Stone Keep, Curtain Wall, Concentric, Courtyard and Gunpowder. For cathedrals we use: Norman, Early-English, Decorated and Perpendicular to describe the styles.

Very few castles or cathedrals are examples of just one style. They were important buildings and were usually modernized from time to time. Spotting these changes is the most important way of understanding any castle or cathedral. Source B is a plan from a modern guidebook. Shading has been used to show when different bits were built. Source C shows part of the same castle. The plan was largely worked out by carefully studying the stonework and spotting the changes.

FitzScrob

Richard FitzScrob may well have been the first person to build a castle in England. Edward the Confessor lived in Normandy before becoming king in 1042. Some Norman friends and supporters came with him when he took the English crown. A leader of this group was Ralph, Earl of Hereford. Ralph was responsible for stopping the Welsh raiding across the border in the area around Hereford.

Richard FitzScrob was one of his followers. It is thought that he came to England in 1052 and built a motte and baily castle – now called Richard's Castle – which is not far from Hereford.

1.2 How do we Know?

Historians use all sorts of things, called **sources**, to tell them about the past. These sources become **evidence** when they are used to support a statement. For example, the picture on this page is a source. But we can also use it as evidence to support the claim that by 1326 the crossbow had been invented.

Historians usually divide sources into two types: primary and secondary. A **primary source** comes from the time you are studying. A **secondary source** usually comes from a later time and, most importantly, it is based on other sources. As we are studying medieval castles and cathedrals the two sources in this Unit are primary sources.

There are lots of different types of primary sources. Some are written and some are not. In this book you will use three main types of non-written primary sources. **Buildings**, the remains of the castles and cathedrals, are the most important. **Archaeology**, the excavation of remains under the ground, is very useful in showing us how sites have changed. Finally, the **art** from the medieval period tells us what things once looked like.

Written primary sources are not always from books. An inscription on a stone tablet is just as much a written source as a manuscript. Sometimes the financial accounts from a castle or cathedral have survived. These show us how many workers were employed, how much they were paid, how much the materials cost and lots more. We are not usually that lucky, though. Sometimes there are descriptions of castles or cathedrals in history books written at the time (called **Chronicles**).

A

SOURCE

Women defending a castle with a bow and a crossbow. From an English manuscript made in 1326.

There is much more to being an historian than just collecting sources. The sources also have to be **interpreted**, to see what they really mean. Then you have to decide whether they are **reliable** – whether you should believe them or not.

Both the sources in this Unit need to be thought about carefully. What does Source A tell us?

- That castle walls were not much taller than the average woman?
- That castles were defended by women who used flowers as missiles?

Obviously not. We can learn useful things from it, though. For a start there are at least five special features you will learn about which are shown in the picture. It tells us that each of these was certainly known about and used by 1326.

William of Malmesbury

William of Malmesbury (died about 1143) is a good example of a **chronicler** – a man who wrote chronicles. He was a monk in Malmesbury Abbey for almost all of his life. He wrote that 'the blood of two races' was mixed in his veins, so he probably had one Saxon and one Norman parent. In his histories he tried to get at the truth and to be fair to both sides. This, for instance, is what he wrote about Harold at the battle of Hastings in 1066:

> *Harold was not content just to be the general and encourage others to fight. He diligently entered into every soldier-like office. Often he would strike the enemy when coming to close quarters, so that nobody could safely come near him, for immediately the same blow would level both horse and rider. ... The battle was not won while Harold was still alive. But, when he fell, from having his brain pierced with an arrow, the English began to fly.*

William was sent to the abbey while he was still a boy, which was the usual practice at the time. He spent the rest of his life as a monk of Malmesbury. This does not mean he spent all his life in the Abbey. He visited the libraries in many other parts of England and he was at the royal court during some of the most important events in the 1130s and 1140s.

B **SOURCE**

Arnold, Lord of Ardres, built on the Motte of Ardres a wooden tower, better than all the other towers of Flanders both in material and in carpenter's work.

On the Ground Floor were cellars and granaries, and great boxes, barrels, casks, and other domestic utensils.

On the first floor were the living rooms, the rooms of the bakers and butlers, and the Great Chamber in which the Lord and his wife slept. Next to this was the dormitory of the waiting maids and children. In the inner part of the Great Chamber was a certain private room, where at early dawn, or in the evening, or during sickness, or for warming the maids and weaned children, they used to have a fire.

On the upper floor were garret rooms in which, on the one side the sons (when they wished) and on the other side the daughters (because they were obliged) of the Lord of the House used to sleep. On this floor also the watchmen appointed to guard the house took their sleep. High up on the east side of the house was the chapel.

There were stairs and passages from floor to floor, from the house into the kitchen, and from room to room.

From a description of the tower of a motte and bailey castle by Lambert d'Ardres, written in the 11th century.

1.3 Christianity and the Middle Ages

The spread of Christianity

ICELAND

NORWAY

SWEDEN

DENMARK

RUSSIA

BRITAIN

POLAND

FRANCE

PORTUGAL

SPAIN

Historians are most interested in explaining **why** things happened in the way that they did. As history is about people in the past, people play an important part in the explanations.

The people who built castles and cathedrals did not have exactly the same ideas as us. Some of the things they thought were important are not the same as the things we think are important. In order to understand why they did things, we need to know about what they thought was important.

In the medieval period Britain was part of **Christendom**. This was the community of Christian people led by the Pope at the head of the Church. It covered most of what we now call Europe. **The Church** was the name given to all Christians, not just to the building in which they worshipped. Everyone in Christendom who was baptized, was a part of this Church.

As Christians, people tried to live good lives. When they died, they hoped to go to **heaven** to be with God for ever. They believed only saints led perfect lives and went straight to heaven.

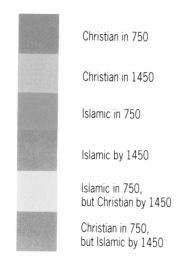

Christian in 750

Christian in 1450

Islamic in 750

Islamic by 1450

Islamic in 750, but Christian by 1450

Christian in 750, but Islamic by 1450

Most people had to spend some time in **purgatory** which was like hell. There they suffered until they had served out their sentences and could go to heaven. People who had lived bad lives, or who did not believe in God, went to **hell** for ever.

By the Middle Ages, most people in Britain believed in Christianity. There were about 9,000 parish churches. These were often very small buildings in very small villages. In towns, there were several parish churches depending on how many people lived there. Going to church meant praying and listening to services. This helped people to lead good lives, to be sorry for things they had done wrong, and to be forgiven by God. People believed that if they gave land or money to the church they would spend less time in purgatory.

The **cathedrals** were huge churches, built to praise God. Services were held all day, every day. Saints were buried in the cathedrals and people came from miles around to pray to a saint. People prayed for help to get them to heaven or to become well, or for a sick loved one to become well.

A

A picture of hell from about 1400.

Breakspear

Nicholas Breakspear, (1100?–59) was the only English Pope there has ever been. His father was said to have been a poor man, who left his family to become a monk at St Albans. Nicholas went to France and became an Augustinian friar. He was made a cardinal in 1146 and sent to Scandanavia to look after the churches there. He returned in 1154 and was elected Pope under the name of Adrian IV.

Adrian was Pope during the time when the Emperor Frederick Barbarossa, who controlled a large empire in Europe, tried to extend his power over Italy. Adrian's reign was taken up with struggles to resist this.

Adrian is remembered in his own country for giving Henry II permission to conquer Ireland. All parts of Ireland that became Christian were to belong to the Pope.

2.1 Castles and the Norman Conquest

In 1066, the **Battle of Hastings** was fought in the south-east corner of England, within a few miles of the coast. It was not the end of the Norman Conquest of England. There was a lot of country left for William to capture.

It took William several years to make himself secure as the king of the whole country. Even when the Normans had taken control of an area, there was often a rebellion against them. Also, there were not very many Normans and their soldiers.

As the Normans took over their new lands they had a pressing need. They needed to be safe – quickly. This applied both to the king and to the knights given lands in reward for fighting in William's army. For all of them the answer was the same – build castles.

A castle was designed to keep the people inside it safe. It was much easier to defend than to attack so a few people inside would be fairly safe even when attacked by many more people outside. This was exactly what the Normans needed.

Most of the first castles that were built were **motte and bailey** castles (see pages 12–13). They were very quick to build, despite the large mound of earth which is their main feature. As soon as William landed, he built one at Hastings. Some parts of this castle were made in Normandy before he sailed and were not put together until it was finally built. The whole job took only seventeen days.

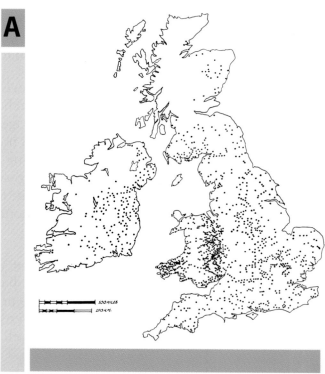

A

The sites of mottes in the British Isles, from 'The Norman Castle' by Derek Renn, 1973.

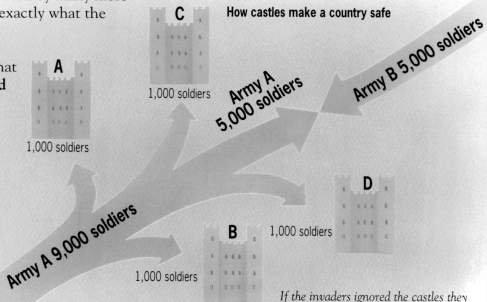

How castles make a country safe

C — 1,000 soldiers
A — 1,000 soldiers
B — 1,000 soldiers
D — 1,000 soldiers
Army A 5,000 soldiers
Army B 5,000 soldiers
Army A 9,000 soldiers

If the invaders ignored the castles they could be attacked from behind. Also, once the invaders had passed the castles, their messengers and supplies could be captured by the soldiers from the castles. To avoid this, they either had to waste time capturing each castle, or leave enough men to besiege them.

Castles can be divided into two types. **Royal Castles** were built by the king and **garrisoned** by royal troops. They usually guarded important towns. **Baronial Castles** were built and lived in by William's followers. They were usually in the baron's lands.

Within a few years of the Battle of Hastings, there were castles all over England. Before 1066 there had been only three or four, built by Normans who had settled here in the time of Edward the Confessor. The Normans thought one of the reasons why they conquered England so easily was because there were not many castles. Not only did castles keep the people who lived in them safe, they also made the whole country safer. The diagram on page 10 shows how this worked. Having castles also made it easier for the Normans to control their new land. From their safe base in the castle, Norman troops could control all the countryside within half a day's ride (about 20 miles).

Norman castles in south-east England

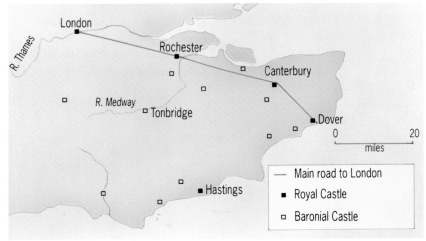

William I

William I (1027?–87) was the eldest son of Robert, Duke of Normandy. In 1035 Robert died while he was on a pilgrimage to Jerusalem. William became Duke, although still a child. It was a difficult time. William had three guardians, all of whom were killed in plots and rebellions.

In the late 1040s and 1050s William won control of his lands. He crushed all resistance to his rule inside Normandy and won lands from the surrounding countries. He visited England in 1051. This was when Edward the Confessor may have promised him the throne.

After 1066 William was a determined, ruthless and successful King of England. He died from an injury he got while fighting in Normandy.

Building the motte at Hastings, from the Bayeux Tapestry.

2.2 Motte and Bailey Castles

Motte and bailey castles, as the name suggests, had two distinct parts. The **motte** was a mound of earth with steep sides and a flat area on top. This was the safest place in the castle because it was the hardest to attack. Around the top of the motte was a fence, and inside this fence a wooden house or tower. The motte was reached by a bridge which connected with a gateway in the fence.

The **bailey** was a larger area, usually level with the ground and protected by a ditch and bank, with another fence on top. There was much more space in the bailey. It was used for larger living accommodation and storage of goods and animals.

The motte and bailey castles were quick and cheap to build. Their greatest weakness was to an attack by fire. There were other problems, too. The top of the motte was usually not very large, so there was not much living space in the tower. Also, the wood they were made from rotted in time, so they would need rebuilding anyway. In the long term they were replaced by stone castles. Often an old motte can still be seen as part of a later stone castle.

B SOURCE

They would heap up a mound of earth as high as they were able, and dig round it a broad, open, deep ditch. They ringed the top of the mound with a barrier of wooden planks, stoutly fixed together with numerous turrets set round. Within was constructed a house, or rather a citadel, commanding the whole. The gate could only be approached by a bridge which was gradually raised as it advanced, crossing the ditch so as to reach the top of the mound level with the gate.

From a description of the motte at Merchem (in France) by Jean de Colmien, written about 1100.

The motte at Bayeux, from the Bayeux Tapestry.

A SOURCE

ENIT: BAGIAS

An attack on the motte and bailey castle at Dinan, from the Bayeux Tapestry.

Odo

Odo (died 1097) was a half-brother of William I. In 1049 William made him Bishop of Bayeux. Some of the men William made bishops were great men of the Church. Others, like Odo, were better known as warriors. Odo played an important part in the battle of Hastings. He was made Earl of Kent and was one of the two men left to run England when William went back to Normandy in 1067. He was very unpopular because he was very harsh, and because he built so many castles. Until 1052 he was the second most important man in England.

Odo spent the last four years of William's reign as a prisoner. He rebelled against William II and was driven out of England. Some historians think he may have ordered the making of the Bayeux Tapestry.

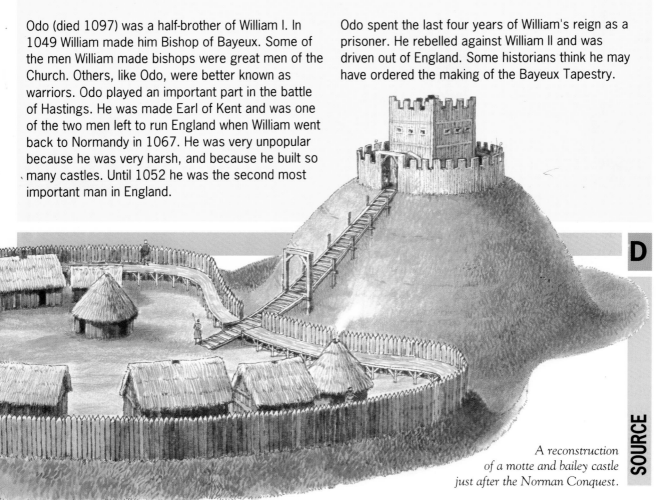

A reconstruction of a motte and bailey castle just after the Norman Conquest.

2.3 Square Keep Castles

From the very first stage of the conquest, the Normans built some stone castles. Any castle showed Norman power, especially if part of a town was knocked down to make the space to build it. Great stone **keeps** built in the most important places, such as the Tower of London, showed just how powerful the Normans were.

Like the motte, the keep was the safest part of the castle. Square keeps were safe because of the strength of their walls, often up to 5 metres thick. This meant they were too heavy to build on mottes. As the strength of the keep was the walls which kept attackers out, special care had to be taken with the doorway and the windows. To make the door safe it was usually on the first floor, reached by a ramp or staircase outside the keep. Usually this ramp went only as far as the **forebuilding**, an extension on the side of the keep to cover the door. It would have been safest not to have had windows. But this would have made the keep too dark to live in. Instead, they made very small **slit windows** near the ground. Arrows could be fired out of these windows, but as they were narrow, nobody outside could climb in through one. Only high up the walls of the keep were windows allowed to get much wider.

Obviously not all keeps were the same size, but they usually followed a similar plan. On the ground floor was storage space, and above this a Great Hall, perhaps two stories high, where most people lived. Between the ground floor and the Great Hall there might be another floor with offices and more living space. Above the Great Hall there was sometimes a floor with more sleeping space – although most people would have slept in the Great Hall.

Square keep castles had weaknesses. There was not much the defenders could do to fight back, unless the doorway was attacked. Usually attackers tried to starve the defenders out or **undermine** the wall so part of it would collapse. The square corners were weak against this type of attack.

Gundulf

Gundulf (1024–1108) is a good example of the energy of the Normans who came to England with William. He was a monk and a friend of Lanfranc whom William made Archbishop of Canterbury. Gundulf was made Bishop of Rochester in 1077. He re-built the Cathedral and also turned it into a monastery. He also built castles. The most famous of these is the Tower of London, where he built the keep which still stands.

A

SOURCE

The keep of Rochester Castle, begun in 1127.

A reconstruction of the keep of Rochester Castle

Stairs, small rooms, and guarderobes (toilets) in the thickness of the walls.

Thick walls, the main defence against any attack.

Turrets giving extra firing positions.

Windows. They get wider the further off the ground they are, so there is less danger of an attacker reaching them to climb in.

Good firing positions from the roof of the forebuilding down onto attackers on the ramp.

Forebuilding, to protect the entrance.

A chapel.

Living space.

A batter. The lowest section of the wall slopes outwards. This had several advantages: the wall was thicker; it was on an angle so battering rams would bounce off; things dropped from the walls would bounce off at the attackers; it kept attackers further away and gave a better angle of fire for defenders on the walls.

The Great Hall, much taller than the other floors, with two sets of windows and a gallery running round the top.

Working and living space.

Storage space.

Entrance through the forebuilding. If the attackers got into the forebuilding there would not be space to use a battering ram on the second door, and they could not fire at it from outside as it was hidden around the corner.

A gap, usually crossed by a drawbridge. When the castle was attacked, the drawbridge was raised and it was another obstacle to get through.

Turret, with two portcullises, to guard the ramp.

Ramp to the forebuilding. Overlooked and fired on from the keep.

2.4 The Normans and the Church

When William invaded England in 1066, he came to a country that had been Christian for 400 years. There were monasteries, convents, churches and cathedrals.

The first Christian missionaries to the Anglo-Saxons had found England divided into a number of small kingdoms. The old Anglo-Saxon **dioceses** (the areas taken care of by each bishop) tended to fit in with the boundaries of these old kingdoms. This was because as the Anglo-Saxon kings became converted to Christianity, so they granted rights to the missionaries to become bishops. These rights only existed within their kingdoms. The bishops often built their cathedrals in quiet country places.

What William brought to England was a strong desire to rule and a great archbishop called **Lanfranc**. Lanfranc was an Italian who trained in law and then in theology. He taught in Normandy where he attracted William's attention. In 1070, William asked him to become Archbishop of Canterbury.

William also appointed other educated Norman bishops in England and Wales. He and Lanfranc encouraged them to build cathedrals in towns and cities. In this way they could look after the souls and lives of many people. There was another reason too. William was fighting to control England. He needed the help and support of the Church. So he wanted his bishops to be loyal to him and to build their cathedrals where most people lived. There they would have more influence over the people. The Pope had supported William in 1066. William now expected the Church in England to tell the people to obey him as God's choice as the rightful king.

A

SOURCE

William required the abbey of Peterborough to produce 60 knights, fully armed horsemen, to serve in the king's army.

From a medieval Chronicle.

Dioceses in England and Wales in the Middle Ages.

The building of Westminster Abbey in 1066, from the Bayeux Tapestry.

Now he laid the foundations of his church with large square blocks of dark stone. In the centre he raises a tower and two at the West Front. The pillars and cornices are rich without and within. From the bases to the capitals the work rises grand and royal.

A description of Westminster Abbey in 1065 from Anglo-Norman verses written in 1245, when the old abbey was being demolished.

Lanfranc

Lanfranc (1005?–89) began his career as a lawyer in Italy. While still young he went to France. In 1039 he became the master of the cathedral school at Avranches in Normandy. After three years he decided to become a monk and entered the monastery at Bec where he set up a school. He became Archbishop of Canterbury in 1070, and made many reforms. He wanted priests to be well educated and to keep their vows. He insisted that the Archbishop of Canterbury was seen as more powerful than the Archbishop of York.

2.5 Norman Cathedrals

A

Peterborough Cathedral. Notice the round arches.

The Norman style of building was very strong-looking. This was partly because the Norman builders did not really understand how strong the stone was with which they worked. The walls of their cathedrals were very thick. This meant they could be built very tall and could take the weight of the roof. Small windows meant that the walls were not weakened by having large holes in them. The large wall space was also ideal for wall paintings.

There was another reason for the thick walls. People looked to cathedrals as places of safety. Like Norman castles, their thick walls and small windows were easy to defend.

B

The monks of Peterborough heard it said that Hereward and his band of rebels against William, meant to plunder the monastery. This was because they heard it said that the king had made a Norman called Turold Abbot, and, that he was a hard man and that he had come with all his Norman followers. Hereward and his outlaws came with many ships. The monks withstood them but the outlaws burnt all the monks' houses and all the town but one house.

From 'The Anglo-Saxon Chronicle'.

C

In spring 1076 William went away over the sea to Normandy and took with him Archbishop Stigand, Abbot Aethelnoth of Glastonbury and many other good men of England. Bishop Odo (the king's half brother) and other Normans remained here, built castles and oppressed the people.

From 'The Anglo-Saxon Chronicle'.

Inside the cathedral, huge pillars helped to hold up the roof. Each block of stone pressed on the one below. The joints were held together by this pressure. The block at the bottom of the pillar took the most weight. No cathedral has ever fallen down because the blocks of stone have been crushed to dust by the weight above.

The Normans used **round arches** for windows and doorways. This was copied from the Roman way of building. In the round arch, the stones fit in like wedges so they cannot fall downwards. The round arch of stones is stronger than a flat piece of stone above a doorway. It can span a wider space. However, the round arch was not strong enough to span right across the **nave** of a cathedral. Flat wooden roofs were used.

There are still some cathedrals today that are mainly Norman. They are at St Albans, Rochester, Durham, Norwich and Peterborough.

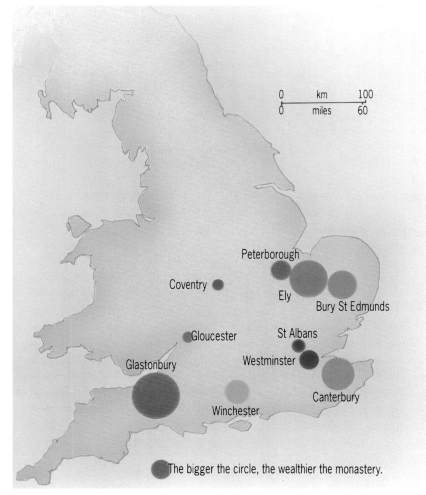

The bigger the circle, the wealthier the monastery.

Hereward

No one knows when Hereward the Wake was born or when he died – many historians see him as a mythical figure. He was an Anglo-Saxon who fought William the Conqueror. There are many legends about him.

In 1070, Hereward was sure the King of Denmark would try to conquer England. Hereward, with his followers and some Danish sailors, decided to attack Peterborough where William the Conqueror had appointed a Norman abbot called Turold. Turold had brought his Norman followers to Peterborough, instead of giving jobs to the native English. Many of the English hated Norman rule anyway, and Turold's actions made them even more resentful.

In fact, the Danish king did not invade England. Hereward had to fly for his life. He fled to the Isle of Ely which became a refuge for Anglo-Saxon rebels against William. William finally captured Ely, but Hereward escaped and nothing more was ever heard of him.

This map shows the value of the wealthiest monasteries and convents at the time of the Domesday Book, 1086.

3.1 The Castle Develops

Not all castles had square keeps. In many places the castle builders decided not to abandon the motte. Instead they built a **shell keep**. The outer wooden wall around the top of the motte was replaced by a stone wall. Rooms were built against the inside of this wall (see Source A).

The shell keep did not need thick walls, as it still had the protection of the motte. Although the living space was bigger, and the stone castle safer, shell keeps were not ideal. It was not convenient to live on top of the motte, and it was still rather cramped.

Round keeps were another style of castle. They were built on the ground (not the motte) and were a development of the square keep castle. The idea was to avoid the weakness of the square corners (see page 14) by not having any. In just the same way as many square keeps are in fact rectangles, round keeps were not always circular, some were polygonal (many sided). Medieval builders could not make the round keeps as large as the square ones, so they were often cramped.

Round and square keeps were usually in the bailey of the castle. The defences of the bailey were improved and the ditch, bank and wooden fence were replaced by a strong stone wall. This was called the **curtain wall** and castles built in this period are called curtain wall castles. At first the curtain wall was not much more than a high stone wall with some firing places and, perhaps, some towers. The idea was that the wall round the bailey should be so strong that the enemy would never get inside the bailey. This meant that both the motte and the keeps started to become less important.

Because the bailey was safer, the buildings in it got more important. Often a Great Hall was built for the lord to live in. As it was not built to be defended it could have thinner walls and much larger rooms and windows.

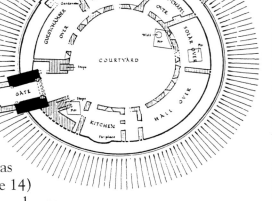

A modern plan of the shell keep at Restormel Castle built about 1200.

The round keep at Pembroke Castle, built about 1200.

C **SOURCE**

Carisbrooke Castle from the air. The shell keep was built by 1136.

Bratticing

Attackers were most dangerous when they were at the foot of the wall. In order to shoot at or even drop things on men at the foot of the wall, defenders had to lean right out, and this made them good targets. Bratticing was a way to get round this problem. It was a wooden extension built out from the top of the wall. It had firing places through the floor and at the front. You can see evidence that Pembroke Castle once had bratticing – there are holes through which the main timbers went.

William Marshal

William Marshal, Earl of Pembroke (1146?–1216), was responsible for building much of Pembroke Castle, including, probably, the round keep. He lived during the reigns of Stephen, Henry II, Richard I, John and Henry III. There were many rebellions against each king, some of which included the heir to the throne, yet through all these reigns Marshal was totally loyal to whoever was king. He was regarded as the 'perfect knight'.

As a boy William was given as a hostage to King Stephen by his father. This did not stop his father rebelling again, but Stephen was so impressed with the boy's bravery he decided not to kill him. When he grew up Marshal was a successful soldier in England, France, Germany and the Holy Land. Once, when Richard I rebelled against his father (Henry II), Marshal could have killed Richard on the battlefield. Instead Marshal killed Richard's horse. When Richard became king, Marshal reminded him of this and Richard did not hold Marshal's loyalty to Henry II against him. Marshal must have been a formidable fighter. In jousting he unhorsed over 500 knights in single combat and when he was over 60 nobody at King John's court would accept a challenge to fight him.

3.2 The Siege of Rochester Castle, 1215

In 1215, King John was at war with many of his leading barons. In June it looked like the barons had won. John had to agree to the **Magna Carta** which gave the barons the rights they were demanding. This was not the end however. John was determined to carry on fighting and win back what he had lost. In September, the barons controlled London and John was in Kent. Rochester Castle, held by the barons, blocked his route to London.

So John besieged Rochester, and captured the city on 11 October. The castle held out until 30 November. First, John's men broke through the curtain wall and captured the bailey. Next, John undermined one corner of the keep. This was a success as the whole corner collapsed. Unfortunately for John, the keep was divided into two and the defenders kept John's men out of half of the keep until they ran out of food.

Methods of besieging a castle

The first decision was whether to starve the castle into defeat, which could take a long time, or capture it by storm, with heavy losses. If there was time, starvation was usually the best policy.

As you can see there were plenty of tactics for storming a castle. Usually more than one would be used at the same time. If there was time to make a **breach** (hole) in the wall, this was usually a good idea.

Battering rams were the simplest way of smashing a wall or door. Often they were used with mobile sheds, called **penthouses** or **sows** to protect the men using the ram from the defenders.

A **belfry** or siege tower could be used in more than one way. Some were kept away from the walls, and used to give a better shooting position into the castle. Others, on wheels, could be pushed up to the castle walls. A drawbridge could be lowered on to the castle wall so that attackers would not have to climb scaling ladders.

There were many types of **stone-throwing engines**. Some were like giant crossbows, others were powered by twisted rope, and others by weights on one end of a pivoted beam. Usually stones were fired at the walls, or over them at the defenders inside the castle. Sometimes other things were fired, like the putrid bodies of dead horses to spread disease inside the castle.

A **mine** was often the best way of damaging a castle. Starting as close to the wall as possible, miners dug a tunnel under the wall itself. The roof of the tunnel was held up with wooden props. When the time was right these were set on fire with the hope that, without the props, the tunnel and the wall above it would collapse.

The king did not allow the besieged any rest day or night. For, amidst the stones hurled from the engines, and the missiles of the crossbows and archers, frequent assaults were made by knights and their followers, so that when some were tired, other fresh ones succeeded them in the assault; and with these changes the besieged had no rest.

The besieged, too, tried to delay their own destruction. They were in great dread of the cruelty of the king. Therefore, that they might not die unavenged, they made no small slaughter amongst the attackers. The siege was prolonged many days owing to the great bravery and boldness of the besieged, who hurled stone for stone, weapon for weapon, from the walls on the enemy.

At last, after great numbers of royal troops had been slain, the king, seeing his engines had little effect, employed miners, who soon threw down a great part of the walls. The provisions of the besieged failed them, and they were obliged to eat their horses. The soldiers of the king now rushed to the breaches in the walls, and by constant fierce assaults they forced the besieged to abandon the castle, though not without great loss on their own side. The besieged then entered the keep.

The king then applied his miners to the keep, and having after much difficulty broken through the walls, an opening was made for the attackers. While the king's army were thus employed, they were often forced to retreat from the destruction caused in their ranks by the besieged.

At length, not a morsel of provisions remaining amongst them, the besieged, thinking it would be a disgrace to die of hunger when they could not be conquered in battle, surrendered.

From an account of the siege written between 1230 and 1236 by Roger of Wendover, a monk.

A trebuchet (a stone-throwing engine) using a pivoted beam, being used during a siege. An illustration from a 13th-century manuscript.

King John

John (1167–1216) was the youngest son of Henry II. He was not a successful king, but his poor reputation in history may owe much to his feuds with the Church – churchmen wrote most of the records of his reign.

While his brother Richard was fighting in the Crusades, John rebelled against the regent running England. Richard forgave him this, and many other acts of treachery. As king, John argued with his barons. He lost most of his land in France and fell out so seriously with the Pope that England was put under *Interdict* – expelled from the Catholic Church while John was king. John's quarrels with his barons eventually resulted in the *Magna Carta* which limited the powers of the king. There was a positive side to John's reign. He was the first ruler of England since the Romans to plan and start a new town – Liverpool, founded in 1207.

3.3 Developments in Castle Defence

Castle building was part of an arms race. Attackers developed new ways of attacking and castle builders had to try to stay one jump ahead of them. Sometimes the natural features of the site were the best defence. It would be hard to dig a successful mine under a castle in a marsh, or in the middle of a lake. It would also be hard to use a belfry on a steep slope. Often castles did not have these natural advantages. In these cases the designers had to find other strengths. Could they dig a ditch so that the castle seemed to be on a slope? Could they divert a stream or a river to use water defences?

Goodrich Castle from the air. There was a castle on this site before 1100, but nothing of that castle survives. The castle has building work from the 12th, 13th, 14th, 15th and 16th centuries.

From the late 12th century onwards, many new ideas came back with the men who returned from the Crusades. The sieges of the Crusades were usually short and decided by storm rather than starvation. Castle designers became more interested in ways the defenders could kill attackers during an attempt to storm the castle. They wanted the defenders to be able to hurt the attackers more. The developments shown in this Unit have two things in common. They all gave the defenders fairly safe positions to kill from. Also, they could either be used in new castles or added to old ones to make them stronger.

Towers and flanking fire

Towers were built along the wall, not just at the corners. They stuck out beyond the wall so that archers inside them could fire along the outside of the wall. Round towers were better than square ones, because they were harder to attack and gave a better field of fire. The towers also divided the wall into sections, usually with the only stairs to the bailey inside the towers. This meant that if the enemy got on to one section of wall they could not get down into the castle, or capture other sections of the wall.

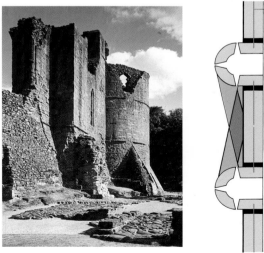

- Wall walk
- ▬ Door or portcullis
- ▦ Field of fire
- Possible fire down from top of tower if attackers capture a section of wall

Machicolations

Machicolations were an alternative to bratticing. They were sections of the wall which jutted out, with holes through them, so that defenders could fire at or drop things on attackers beneath. Because they were built from stone, they were more expensive than bratticing, but could not be set on fire during an attack. They were usually built on sections of the wall which were likely to be attacked. They were often used as part of a barbican (see below).

Attackers eye-view. The machicolations from below.

Carisbrooke Castle, showing barbican and machicolations.

The barbican

This is the name given to the defences built to protect the entrance. Almost every barbican is different, but there are a few common principles. First, find ways of crowding the attackers together in narrow spaces; this makes them a better target. Second, have lots of barriers they have to get past, like moats, drawbridges, portcullises and doors. This slows them down and gives the defenders much longer to kill them. Finally, have lots of well-protected positions to fire on the attackers. The aim was to make the barbican a **killing ground**.

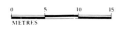

Key

1   An extra defence, with its own gateway and walls. Only from this could attackers get onto the bridge. Overlooked by firing positions on the castle wall and towers.

2   Bridge over deep, dry moat. Attackers crowded together. Overlooked by firing positions on the gatehouse.

3   Drawbridge over dry moat.

4   Long corridor with a series of doors and portcullises. Firing positions from the side and from above (through the ceiling, called **murder holes**).

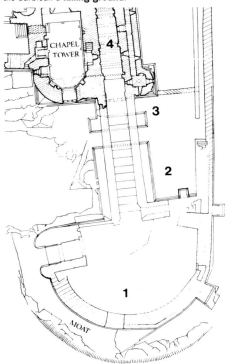

Plan of the barbican at Goodrich Castle.

Countess Isabel

Isabel de Fortibus (died 1293) was the sister and heir of the Earl of Devon. In 1248, she married William de Fortibus, Earl of Albermarle. They had five children. Their sons all died in infancy and only one daughter, Avelina, survived to adulthood. William died in 1260. As was normal at the time, Avelina inherited his estates, not Isabel. Avelina was now the richest heiress in the kingdom. She was married to Edmund, younger son of King Henry III, when she was only 10, but died 4 years later.

Isabel was the richest non-royal woman in England. She made her home at Carisbrooke on the Isle of Wight. This had been part of her father's lands, not her husband's. In the 31 years she lived there, she re-built most of the living accommodation.

3.4 Life in a Castle

We have to work hard to understand what life would have been like in a castle. We have to put together clues from the surviving buildings and a whole range of other sources. Obviously it would have been different at different times between 1066 and 1500. Also, it would have been different for the lord and his family than for a serving man or woman.

It is harder to work out what castles were like to live in than it is to understand how the defences worked in a siege.

In some castles, the keep was the centre of day-to-day life. In others, there was a **Great Hall** and other domestic buildings in the bailey and these were the centre of castle life, unless there was a siege. Often we have to work out what the building was like from the clues in the walls. For instance, the part of the keep you can see in Source A had two floors originally, not one or three. The walls inside the buildings would not have been bare stone, they would have been plastered and painted (like Source C) or covered with wooden panelling.

In the early castles most people would have lived in the Great Hall. The lord and his family may have had one or more private rooms, often called **solars**. There was much less privacy in a castle than we expect today. In 1254, Henry III insisted that a new staircase was built at Rochester because he was fed up with people walking through his bedroom on their way to the chapel.

Toilets were usually called **guarderobes**. Often they were built into thick walls, with chutes for the waste to fall down. Alternatively, they were built jutting out from the wall (like Source B). In either case, something still had to be done with the waste. If possible, the chutes would be over the moat and the water would wash the waste away. If this was not possible a pit would be dug and every so often someone would have to empty it.

SOURCE A

The Great Hall, inside the Keep of Rochester Castle.

SOURCE B

*Guarderobes at Conwy Castle. Building in this way, where something juts out from the wall in stages, is called **corbelling**. It is used for other things in castles, such as making a ledge to rest a floor on inside a building.*

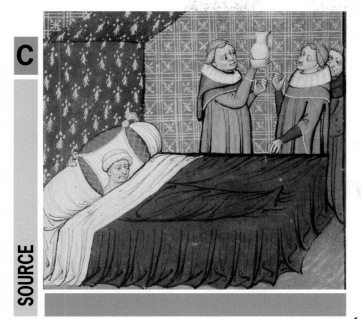

Inside a private chamber, from a 14th-century manuscript.

The 'normal day' would start with an early breakfast, probably eaten in the Great Hall. During the morning most people would work. Lunch, the main meal of the day, was served around noon, again in the Great Hall. Afternoons might be spent hunting or practising knightly skills; spinning, weaving or reading; or still working, depending on your sex and social class.

A visit by the king or a great lord would change the routine. Great feasts would be held. There would be many more people about because important people travelled with large **retinues** of barons and knights.

14	Oxen lying in salt
2	Oxen ffreyssh
120	hedes of shepe fressh
120	carcas of shepe fressh
12	bores
14	calvys
140	pigges
300	maribones
	Larde and Grece ynogh
3	ton of salt Veneson
3	does of ffresh Veneson
50	swannes
210	Gees
59	Capons of hie Grece
8	dozen other Capons
60	dussen Hennes
400	Conyngess
4	Fesuantes
5	Herons and Bitores
6	Kiddes
5	dozen Pullayn for Gely
12	dozen to roast
100	dozen Peions
12	dozen Partrych
8	dozen Rabettes
12	Cranes
	Wilde Fowle ynogh
120	galons melke
12	galons Creme
11	galons Cruddes
12	baskets of Applelles
11	thousand Egges.

The 'shopping list' for a feast given by Richard II and the Duke of Lancaster on 23 September 1387. Unlike most documents in this book, we have kept this one in the original spelling.

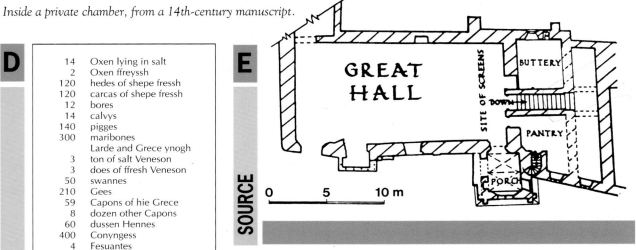

A plan of the Great Hall in the upper bailey of Chepstow Castle.

Richard II

Richard II (1367–1400) became king at just 10 years of age. It was a hard time. The effects of the Black Death and the Hundred Years' War with France had made the country poor. In 1381 the Peasants' Revolt nearly succeeded: London was captured. The turning point came when the 14-year-old Richard rode out to the main body of the peasants after their leader, Watt Tyler, had been killed in front of them. Richard persuaded them to return home without more fighting. This was the high point of his short reign. Most of the promises he made to them he later broke. He was a cultured man, a patron of artists and poets, and a lover of good food and wine.

3.5 Concentric Castles: Buildings to Kill People

The developments covered in Unit 3.3 – machicolations, flanking fire and barbicans – were ways of giving the defenders more chances to kill attackers. The same idea was behind the concentric castle. Concentrated firepower made storming the castle too costly for attackers. The concentric castle used flanking fire, barbicans and machicolations. It also used a new idea, the **concentric principle** – having at least two walls, with the inside one much taller than the outside one.

The first diagram shows how the concentric principle worked. On the outside is a shorter curtain wall. This wall had towers to give flanking fire, and also a wall-walk along the top with plenty of firing positions. Inside this wall, and not all that far away, was a second, much taller curtain wall. From its towers and wall-walk, men could fire over the shorter outside wall at the attackers. The second diagram shows how so many interlocking fields of fire made any approach to the castle a killing ground.

The concentric principle.

Soldiers from Britain had first seen concentric castles on the Crusades. Between the end of the 12th century and the end of the 13th century, the concentric principle was used in a number of British castles. Sometimes they built completely new castles, like Caerphilly. But it was possible to use the concentric idea by adapting an old castle. During the reign of Henry II, two new curtain walls were added to Dover Castle. The second was built outside the first wall. It was shorter and slightly lower down the slope of the hill. This meant that one of the country's oldest castles became again the most up-to-date castle in the land. The Tower of London was also made into a concentric castle with a second, shorter, outer curtain wall.

Defenders had many advantages in concentric castles. Wherever the castle was attacked from, they had lots of firing positions covering the ground. If a section of the outer wall was captured, it could be shut off by closing the entries into the towers.

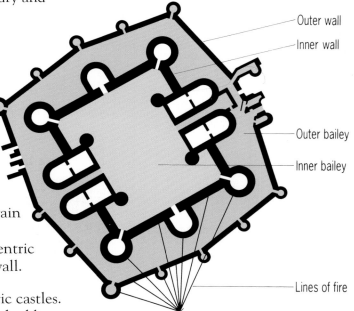

A plan of Beaumaris Castle showing the effect of concentrated firepower.

SOURCE

Dover Castle, showing the concentric effect of Henry II's walls.

Trapped on this section of wall, attackers could be fired on from the inner walls and towers and also the towers in the outer wall. If they managed to get down into the outer bailey they would be crowded into a small space and still be fired on by defenders from the inner wall. The inner wall was a more difficult one to attack, and much harder to use normal siege tactics against. It would be almost impossible to attack using a belfry, for example.

Concentric castles gave the defence more value from each soldier. In older curtain wall castles a large garrison would be needed to cover long stretches of wall. Even if only one part of the castle was attacked it would not be safe to leave sections of the walls without many men, in case they were being tricked. In a concentric castle this was less of a problem. If men were evenly spread around Beaumaris, for example, at least a quarter of them would be involved in any attack. Also, men could be moved quickly around the inner walls to reinforce sections of the castle.

Caerphilly Castle.

B

SOURCE

de Burgh

Hubert de Burgh (died 1243) successfully defended Dover Castle against Louis IX of France and English barons rebelling against King John in 1216. A chronicler has left this description of part of the siege:

> Hubert de Burgh, a brave knight, with 140 knights and a large number of soldiers, destroyed so many of the enemy that the French, feeling their loss, moved their tents and engines further from the castle. Louis was greatly enraged and swore he would not leave the place until the defenders were taken and hung. Louis therefore, to strike terror in them, built a number of shops and other buildings in front of the entrance to the castle, so that the place appeared like a market; for he hoped he would, by hunger and a protracted siege, force them to surrender, as he could not subdue them by force of arms.

The psychological warfare failed. Hubert held out in Dover. The next year he destroyed Louis' chances of victory by turning admiral. Louis had hired a well-known pirate, Eustace the Monk, to command the French navy. Eustace sailed for England with 80 large ships and many smaller ones, bringing Louis a new army. Hubert attacked with a much smaller fleet, captured 55 French ships and sank many more. For most of the rest of his life he was the one king's chief advisors.

3.6 Edward I, Castles & the Conquest of Wales

There was no Norman Conquest of Wales. The borders between England and Wales were called the **Marches**. The Lords of the Marches were encouraged to attack the Welsh whenever they felt like it and to slowly take over the country. By 1272, when Edward I became king, the Marcher Lords controlled all of south Wales and much of the centre. Only the Principality of Gwynedd was ruled by a Welshman, Llywelyn ap Gruffyd. Attempts to conquer Gwynedd had always failed. The Welsh retreated to the mountains of Snowdonia and used guerilla tactics to break the invaders.

In November 1276, King Edward declared war on Llywelyn. He spent the winter planning and raised his army in the spring of 1277. Edward began his campaign from Chester and, in addition to his army, he had a fleet of 27 ships and hundreds of diggers, woodcutters, carpenters, masons and other workers. His plan was to capture the north coast of Wales. This would separate mainland Gwynedd from Anglesey. This would be a great threat to Llywelyn because most of Gwynedd's food was grown in Anglesey.

The first obstacle Edward had to cross was the River Dee. Edward crossed at Flint and stayed there long enough to make a great fortified camp. This became Edward's new fortified town of Flint, and work was soon begun on a castle.

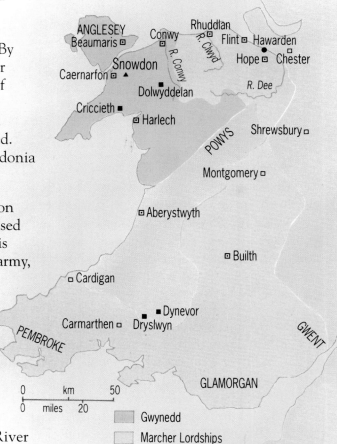

Wales, 1274-1294

- Gwynedd
- Marcher Lordships
- ▣ Castles built or rebuilt by Edward I
- ■ Castles repaired by Edward I
- ▢ Other Royal Castles

0 km 50
0 miles 20

A

Edward I's castle and fortified town at Caernarfon.

SOURCE

Next, Edward crossed the River Clwyd and started a second castle at Rhuddlan. His greatest obstacle was the River Conwy. To make things worse, Llywelyn was waiting with his army on the other bank. Instead of attacking Llywelyn head on, Edward used the fleet to take a strong force to Anglesey. Here they destroyed the harvest and threatened to cross back again to the mainland. This time, they would be behind Llywelyn. With little food, and faced with the prospect of being caught between Edward's army on the River Conwy and the English soldiers from Anglesey, Llywelyn surrendered.

War broke out again in 1282, and lasted for fifteen months. This time the Welsh had some successes attacking the half-finished castles. But Llywelyn and his brother David were both killed in the war and when Edward finally won he annexed all of Gwynedd as crown land. More castles were built to keep it safe at Harlech, Conwy, Caernarfon and Beaumaris. Caernarfon, Conwy, Rhuddlan and Flint all had fortified new towns built alongside the castle. English settlers came to live in them to make the conquest more secure. Conwy Castle was built on the site of Llywelyn's palace and the abbey where his grandfather, Llywelyn the Great, had been buried.

Llywelyn

Llywelyn ap Gruffyd (died 1282) was the last Welsh prince of Wales. He first ruled with his elder bother, Owain, but there was a civil war in 1254 and Owain was defeated, leaving Llywelyn the sole ruler of north Wales. Between 1256 and 1260 Llywelyn increased his lands by attacking the Marcher lords and lands controlled by the English in south Wales. In 1263 he joined in the revolt of Simon de Montfort against Henry III of England. When peace was restored in 1267, after the defeat and death of de Montfort, Llywelyn was acknowledged as the Prince of all Wales, in return for accepting Henry III as his overlord. After Henry died Llywelyn refused to do the same homage to Edward I and began to raid the lands of the Marcher Lords again. This led to Edward's declaration of war in 1276 and the defeat of Llywelyn in 1277. Llywelyn was forced to accept Edward as his overlord, but he did keep his control of Snowdonia and Anglesey. The next year Edward was present at Llywelyn's wedding to Eleanor, the daughter of Simon de Montfort. Eleanor died in giving birth to her their only child, a daughter, in 1282. Later that year Llywelyn was at war with Edward again. As in 1277 Llywelyn was trapped in the mountains of Snowdonia as winter approached. This time, instead of surrendering, he broke out with a small force, only to be caught and killed by English soldiers on 11 December.

Edward I's Welsh castle building was a massive operation. The biggest in Britain since the Normans had built so many castles in the years after 1066. The ten great castles were all Royal Castles. This meant they were paid for from the king's money. Even in the 13th century there were a lot of civil servants to organize the royal finances and civil servants usually need to write things down. As a result we know quite a lot about the building of these castles.

Various types of documents have survived in the royal papers:
- Letters from the king to those in charge of the work in Wales.
- Letters and commands from the royal government to sheriffs in different parts of the country. These were usually about collecting and sending building materials and people to the castle sites.
- Accounts from each of the sites about how much was paid to each worker or group of workers, how much was spent on materials etc.
- General accounts about how much was spent on each site each year.

Unfortunately we do not have all the papers. Many have survived, but some have not.

Edward chose **James of St George** as the chief architect for all of the castles in Wales. They had probably first met in Savoy in 1273, when Edward was on his way home from a Crusade. St George had already built several castles in Savoy, and Edward must have been impressed with his work. Edward called him to England in 1277, when he began to plan the Welsh campaign. Soon St George was Master of the King's Works in Wales, paid the huge sum of 3 shillings (15p) a day, with a pension of 1s 6d (7p) for his widow should he be killed. He planned all of Edward's Welsh castles and often supervised the building work. When he did, costs were always lower than when he didn't. St George also used his skills to destroy castles, and he was the Chief Engineer in Edward's later campaigns in France and Scotland, where he was in charge of siege works.

B SOURCE

Building techniques, from a 13th-century manuscript.

C SOURCE

Edward must have been delighted with the design for 'the new castle at Beau Mareys' and he pressed the work ahead fast. During the summer of 1295, under the protection of the fleet, about 1,800 diggers were at work on the site, plus 450 masons and 375 quarrymen – coins from their wages still occasionally turn up in the neighbourhood. Some 2,300 trees were felled to provide timber, and among other items we hear of 2,428 tons of coal (for the forges) and 105,000 assorted nails.

From 'The National Trust Book of British Castles' by Paul Johnson, 1978.

D Writs were sent all over England to sheriffs, instructing them to find and send workmen. Thus the sheriffs of Gloucestershire, Devon, and Hampshire were each to send 60 'good' masons. The sheriffs of Somerset and Dorset were each to find 120 masons and 40 'good' carpenters, and ship them to Aberystwyth. But these were target figures. Somerset and Dorset sent 80 masons, but no carpenters; Gloucester produced only 47 masons, Wiltshire 27, and Hampshire none at all. Only Devon produced more masons than it was asked.

From 'The National Trust Book of British Castles' by Paul Johnson, 1978.

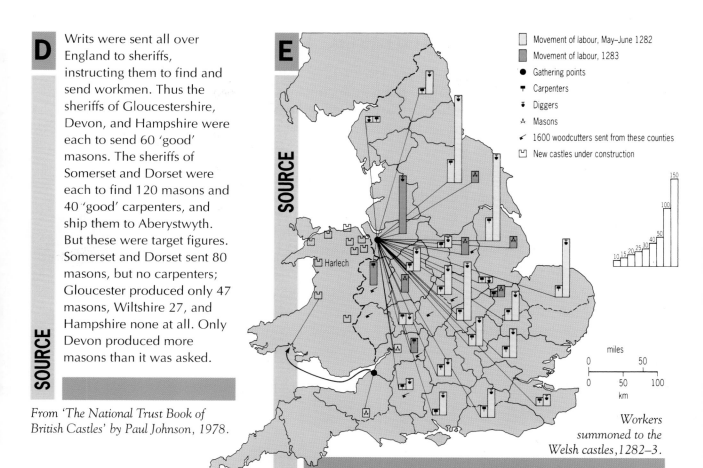

E

Key:
- Movement of labour, May–June 1282
- Movement of labour, 1283
- Gathering points
- Carpenters
- Diggers
- Masons
- 1600 woodcutters sent from these counties
- New castles under construction

Workers summoned to the Welsh castles, 1282–3.

Edward I

Edward I (1239–1307) was born to special rejoicing, for it had been feared that his mother was unable to have children. He had several serious illnesses as a child, but survived them. In 1252 his father gave him Gascony to rule. In 1254 Edward was married to Eleanor, the sister of Alfonso X of Castille. Henry gave them control of lands in Ireland, Wales and several important towns as a wedding gift.

Edward I set about taking control of the lands he had been given, and is famous for his long and successful struggle to subdue the Welsh. The castles that he built to keep the Welsh under control were a constantly visible sign of his power.

As he died he ordered that his body should not be buried until the Scots, who he had been fighting, were beaten. His orders were disobeyed.

Edward I's Castlebuilding in Wales			Royal castles rebuilt	Non-royal castles influenced
New royal castles				
Builth	Ruthin	Caernarfon	Dolwyddelan	Denbigh
Aberystwyth	Hope	Beaumaris	Criccieth	Hawarden
Flint	Conwy		Bere	Holt
Rhuddlan	Harlech			Chirk

4.1 Durham – a Monastic Cathedral

Although William conquered England in 1066, by 1080 he still did not fully control the north of England. So he appointed William of St Calais as Prince Bishop of Durham. He was both a prince with royal power to command an army and he was a religious leader.

He was so powerful that in 1088 he was accused of plotting against the new king, William Rufus. He was exiled but brought back three years later. When he returned to Durham he pulled down the old Saxon cathedral. In August 1093, Prince Bishop William and Prior Turgot watched the foundations of the present cathedral being laid.

Jobs in a monastic cathedral

Bishop in overall charge of the monastic cathedral

Prior in charge of the monks

Chancellor in charge of the library

Precentor responsible for the music

Sacrist responsible for maintaining the buildings

Bursar in charge of the money and monastery supplies

Cellarer responsible for the food and drink

Hostillar responsible for the guests

Chamberlain responsible for the monks' clothing

Refectorian in charge of the dining hall

Master of the infirmary responsible for caring for the old and sick monks

Almoner in charge of the school and of giving help to the poor

Granator responsible for the buying and storage of grain (wheat, barley, oats, rye etc.)

A

SOURCE

A 12th-century illustration of St Dunstan. He is wearing a white **pallium** with little crosses on it. This shows he is an archbishop.

Durham was always a **monastic** cathedral. Of the nineteen cathedrals in England in the Middle Ages, ten were monasteries. The other nine were **secular** cathedrals. These were run by ordinary clergy (see page 39).

In monastic cathedrals the monks lived communally, eating in refectories and sleeping in dormitories. They did not own anything and could not leave the monastery for any reason without the prior's permission. The prior was in charge of the monks.

Plan of Durham Cathedral in the Middle Ages.

North transept
Sacrist's checker
High altar
North church door
North aisle
Cathedral nave
Rood screen
Choir
Bishop's throne
South aisle
Spendement
Garden and bowling alley for the novices
Dormitory stairs
Cloister garth
Common house
Dormitory
Well
Conduit
Vestry
South transept
Parlour (library over)
Chapter house
St. Cuthbert's shrine
Cemetery garth
Prison
Rere-dorter (latrines)
Great cellar
Cellar
Loft
Refectory
Site of the infirmary
Yard
Coal garth
Prior's lodging
Prior's chapel
Cellarer's checker
Kitchen
Bursar's checker
Prior's hall
Prior's solar
Chamberlain's checker
School
Guest hall
Priory garth
Great gate
N
South bailey
Granaries

0   15   30
metres

St Cuthbert

Cuthbert (died 687) became Bishop of Lindisfarne, off the Northumberland coast. He lived a more and more solitary life, eventually living on a small island nearly, and seeing no one. After his death he was brought back to Holy Island and buried there. Eleven years later his body was dug up to be re-buried above ground, and the monks said it had not decayed at all. When the Danes raided in 875, some of the monks escaped, taking his coffin with

them. After being carried from place to place for about two hundred years, the coffin was brought to Durham Cathedral. Cuthbert's body was believed to work miracles, so many pilgrims came to his shrine. It is said that every time masons tried to build a Lady Chapel near Cuthbert's tomb, it fell down, because he disliked women. That is why the Lady Chapel at Durham is at the west end of the Cathedral – the opposite end to the shrine.

In the middle of the 12th century, new methods of building were developed in France. The French were building with thinner walls. Their churches were taller and lighter. The new churches soared upwards to the heavens, letting the light in from above.

This style of building quickly spread. Much later this style was called **Gothic**. In England the first phase of Gothic was called **Early-English**. The main features of this style were:

- The pointed arch
- The flying buttress
- The ribbed vault

All of these features had already been used in some cathedrals. However, in Early-English cathedrals they were used together.

The flying buttress supported the walls and stopped them falling outwards.

A

The nave of Durham Cathedral, looking east.

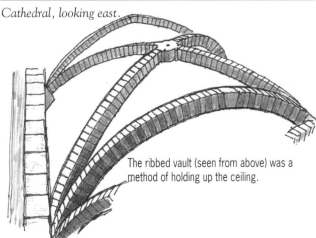

The ribbed vault (seen from above) was a method of holding up the ceiling.

In 1174, a bad fire damaged the east end of Canterbury Cathedral. It was rebuilt by a Frenchman, William of Sens, in the new style. William of Sens was a man of great abilities and a most ingenious workman in wood and stone. And he, residing many days with the monks carefully surveying the burnt walls did yet for some time conceal what he found necessary to do, lest the truth should kill us in our hopelessness. But he went on preparing all things that were necessary. And when he found that the monks began to be somewhat comforted, he confessed that the damaged pillars and all that they supported must be destroyed, if the monks wished to have a safe and excellent building. At length they agreed. Attention was given to get stones from abroad. He made the most ingenious machines. He delivered also to the masons models for cutting the stones. (Five years later William fell 50 feet when scaffolding gave way. He continued to give orders from his bed.) At length, finding no benefit from the skill of his surgeons, he went to France to die at home.

From the Chronicles of Gervase, written by a monk at Canterbury in the 12th century.

The east end of Canterbury Cathedral.

de Eastry

Henry de Eastry (died 1331) was prior of the monastery associated with Canterbury Cathedral for over forty years. He was good at managing money. He paid off the monastery's debts, increased the rents on their lands and raised enough money for the Cathedral rebuilding to be continued. (It had been badly damaged in a fire in 1174.) He bought many books for the library.

4.3 Early-English

The most complete Early-English cathedral is Salisbury. It was built from start to finish in 38 years (1220–1258). So it is all in one style of architecture. The old Norman cathedral had shared the hill of Old Sarum with the Norman castle. This had never been satisfactory. The cathedral, bishop and clergy occupied about a quarter of the space inside the bailey of the castle. There were not enough houses for the clergy. The hill was short of water. The wind was terrible so the clergy complained that they could hardly hear themselves sing and they suffered from rheumatism. Worst of all the cathedral was in the line of fire from the castle and was continually damaged.

Salisbury Cathedral, with the hill of Old Sarum in the background. The canons lived in the houses around the green.

A

So in 1217, the bishop, Richard Poore, asked the Pope if he could move the cathedral into the valley. There was certainly no shortage of water there. Salisbury Cathedral was built where two rivers flow into the River Avon. A river runs below the cathedral so there was no crypt (underground area). The foundations were only 1.2 metres deep and went down to a gravel bed in the river. If the cathedral had been built 70 metres in any direction, it would have sunk long ago.

Salisbury was a **secular** cathedral. This meant that it did not have a monastery attached to it. The men who said the services and ran the cathedral were secular clergy, not monks. They were called **canons**. They lived separately in private houses around the cathedral. They were allowed to own property and could travel about quite freely. In the later Middle Ages some of the canons did not even live in Salisbury. They took their incomes from the cathedral and then paid a minor clergyman or vicar to say their services every day.

The **Dean and Chapter** met in the Chapter House every day. The Chapter consisted of the Dean (President), the Chancellor (secretary and responsible for the library and school), the Precentor (in charge of music), the Treasurer (responsible for the money) and about twenty other canons (members of the Chapter).

Poore

Richard Poore (died 1237) was dean of Salisbury Cathedral for nineteen years and became bishop in 1217. He asked the Pope's permission to build a new cathedral. The Pope agreed. The abbess of Wilton refused him permission to build on her land, so he built the cathedral on land that belonged to him. On 28 April 1220 he laid five of the foundation stones with his own hands: one for himself, one for the Pope, one for Archbishop Langton, one for Earl William and one for the Countess of Salisbury.

The building of the cathedral was supervised by Elias de Dereham, assisted by a famous master mason called Nicholas of Ely. The building was finished in just 38 years. Poore was made Bishop of Durham in 1228, so he did not stay to see it finished. He was a very learned man, who was liked for his goodness and his ability to organize and inspire other people. Because of his leadership both as dean (when he headed a group of gifted and learned men in the chapter) and as bishop, many scholars were attracted to Salisbury.

4.4 Processions

Processions were a type of religious service and an important part of the Church's year. They were held for great festivals such as Easter or Whitsun. They could also be held on special occasions, to celebrate a victory in war or to ask God to spare the people from some great danger.

Processions were not only held in cathedrals, but cathedrals were the setting for the grandest processions. Processions started down the long nave and round the side aisles. The great West Doors were flung open and out would come the clergy carrying banners and singing. The ordinary people of the town joined in behind them and the procession might wind its way round the town before returning to the cathedral. Each cathedral had its own processions, for example on the day of the patron saint, as well as regular ones.

These processions were a time of celebration. In Exeter Cathedral, the clergy dressed in white for the Easter Procession. In 1470 even the king, who was staying nearby, joined in. The accounts of the Cathedral Chapter show there was a feast after each procession and what the feast cost. Apart from the drink, a large part seems to have been 'the cost of the flans'. These flans were made in the canon's bakery and were made from pastry, cheese, butter, cream, honey, pepper and eggs. They used about 3,000 eggs in the flans each year! The procession held in June each year ended with a huge bonfire on the cathedral green and a mock battle between the Canon's servants.

The picture on these pages is taken from a book called *The Tres Riches Heures of John Duke of Berry*, written in the 15th century. It shows a famous procession in Rome in AD 590. A terrible plague was sweeping through the city. The previous Pope had died from it. People were falling sick and dying in the streets every day. Nothing seemed to stop the spread of the disease. The new Pope, Gregory, assembled a procession of clergy and ordinary people to ask God to spare them from the plague. The story goes that a statue of Archangel Michael was seen replacing his sword in his scabbard. This was a sign that the plague was over.

The artist has set his painting of the procession in the 15th century, not in 590. In 590 the clothes and buildings would have been different. Plagues often hit the crowded cities of medieval Europe. Processions were still held to ask God to spare people from the plague. This is the last page in *The Tres Riches Heures* to be painted by three brothers called Limbourg. They all died suddenly in 1416, probably of the plague.

4.5 The Work of Cathedrals

Cathedrals were built for the worship of God on a grand scale. At both monastic and secular cathedrals, the *Opus Dei* (work of God) went on all day.

Matins started at midnight and took about an hour. It was followed by the service of **Lauds**. Then some of the clergy went back to bed until it was time for the first daytime service – **Prime**. After that, they all went to the Chapter House for a short service, followed by the day's business. This could include work on the buildings, fines for clergy who had missed services, food supplies for the community (often about 70 people), organizing processions and so on. Then it was back to the cathedral for services, the main meal of the day and then more services.

All the services were held in the **choir** of the cathedral. Only the clergy could attend. The ordinary people stood about in the nave. They prayed and listened or treated the nave as a place to meet friends and conduct business.

The day ended at about five o'clock when the clergy went home. The curfew bell rang at nine, warning people to put out their fires and go to bed.

A

SOURCE

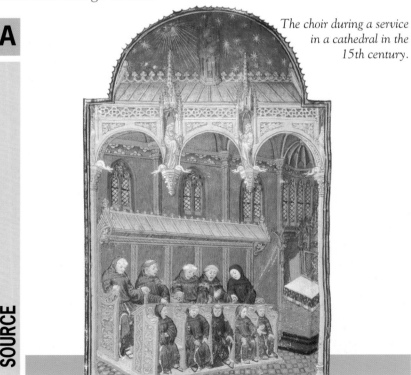

The choir during a service in a cathedral in the 15th century.

B

SOURCE

Passing lately through your diocese we saw many things which we thought we had corrected during our visit – incest, simony, mis-appropriation of churches, children not confirmed. These things need your attention, but you have been absent so long that you seem not to care. We therefore order you, on receipt of this letter, to take up residence in your diocese, so that – even if you are not competent to cure spiritual evils –- you can look after the day-to-day needs of the poor. If you cannot conduct confirmations yourself, you must provide some other bishop to go round the diocese and do what is necessary. Let us hear from you by the Feast of St Thomas the Apostle (21 December) that you have done this.

Letter from John Peckham, Archbishop of Canterbury to Roger Longespee, Bishop of Coventry, 19 November 1282.

'Simony' and 'mis-appropriation of churches' mean paying money to gain the job of being a clergyman, or to gain the income from a church, without providing services and care.

Confirmation is teaching people who have been baptized about the Church so that they can 'confirm' they want to be members of the Christian Church.

Here, overthrown by death, lies William surnamed Wykeham.
He was the bishop of this church and the repairer of it.
He was open handed as the rich and the poor can equally prove.
He was also an able politician and a councillor of the State.
His good work is shown by the colleges which he founded.
The first of which is at Oxford and the second at Winchester.
You who behold this tomb, cease not to pray
That, for such great goodness, he may enjoy eternal life.

Epitaph (words written on the tomb of someone who has died) for William Wykeham, Bishop of Winchester (1367–1404).

In 1330 Bishop Grandisson said of the cathedral clergy that some had 'their bodies in the choir but their hearts in the market place, or the street or still in bed. Worst of all during Matins (the midnight service) the clergy at the back of the choir dropped hot wax on the heads of those below'.

Grandisson was a famous and strict bishop of Exeter Cathedral.

Grandisson

Bishop John Grandisson, (1293–1369) was appointed Bishop of Exeter by Pope John XXII in 1327. He had been a friend of the Pope and his was one of the very few appointments made by the Pope rather than the king.

Grandisson was a very strict disciplinarian and strongly disapproved of laziness. He wrote guidelines on how the Cathedral clergy were to be occupied and have their day filled. He disapproved of jokes which mocked the clergy. He was keen to encourage more people in Britiain to worship saints in the way they did on the continent. Often this involved lavish processions and feasts.

Grandisson was not a rich man but he gave timber from his own estate at Chudleigh for building works at Exeter Cathedral. After he died in 1369, a grand tomb was built in the Cathedral and a huge two-ton bell was struck in his honour.

A 14th-century bellfounder's window in York Minster. Bells were rung for every cathedral service.

4.6 Building the Medieval Cathedral

The setting time of the mortar used in the Middle Ages was very slow and could take as much as a year or a year and a half to set.

From 'The Construction of Gothic Cathedrals' by J. Fitchen, 1981.

The eight oak corner posts for the octagon tower at Ely are each 63 feet (about 7 metres) long and weigh 10 tonnes (about the weight of 10 large cars each). They were brought by water across the fens and had to be lifted 100 feet (about 30 metres) up above the nave.

From 'The Gothic Cathedral' by D. Smith.

Once the decision was taken to build or rebuild a cathedral someone had to organize the work. This was done by the Dean and Chapter. They employed a master **mason**, who was both architect and stone mason. He, in turn, employed masons, often from many miles away. They built a thatched hut or 'lodge' close by the site of the cathedral. The masons lived, slept and ate in this lodge and worked on the plans. They kept themselves apart in order to keep the secrets of their building techniques. They passed their knowledge on to their apprentices, who would one day be full masons.

Carpenters and blacksmiths were needed as soon as work began. The carpenters saw to all the woodwork – from scaffolding, to the roof timbers and the carved choir stalls in the finished cathedral. The blacksmiths made and repaired all the tools.

Building St Albans Cathedral in the 13th century.

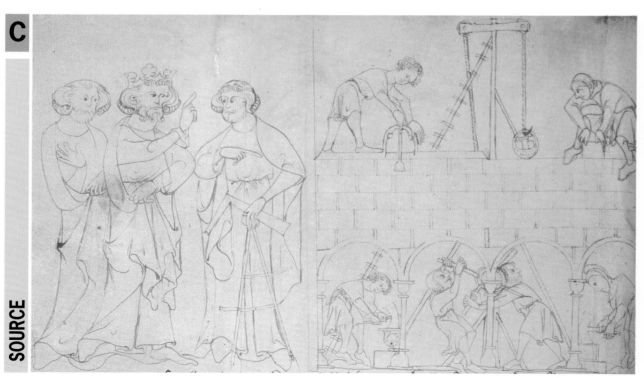

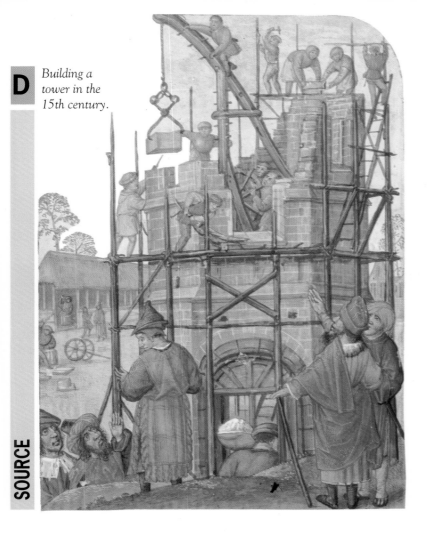

D Building a tower in the 15th century.

SOURCE

de Honnecourt

Villard de Honnecourt (1225?–50) is famous for his sketchbook which shows the ways in which architects worked in the 13th century. He visited many of the great French cathedrals. He is known to have worked on some, such as the rose window at Lausanne.

De Honnecourt's sketchbook shows drawings of figures and technical diagrams. For example it shows how to calculate the circumference of a pillar when most of it is hidden by other stonework. This was useful when masons had to repair cathedrals built perhaps two or three hundred years earlier. He also sketched the cathedrals he visited. His sketchbooks give us insights into cathedral building skills. They also show how much masons travelled in the Middle Ages; they had skills that were in demand everywhere. He does not appear to have come to Britain.

E

SOURCE

Inside the roof of Salisbury Cathedral. Oak was used for the beams and a softer wood for the lattice work, on which the lead roof was placed.

Week	White cutters	Marblers	Layers	Carpenters	Polishers	Smiths	Glaziers	Plumbers	Labourers	Total
June 23-29	53	49	28	28	15	17	14	4	220	428
June 30-July 6	56	49	28	23	15	17	14	4	220	426
July 7-13	60	49	14	21	15	17	13	4	215	408
July 14-20	60	49	14	16	15	17	6	4	215	396
July 21-27	66	49	14	16	15	17	6	4	140	327
July 28-August 3	68	49	14	16	15	16	6	4	130	321
August 4-10	78	49	14	16	15	16	6	4	135	333

Sometimes the roof of the cathedral was tiled, but often it was made out of sheets of lead. These were put in to place by the plumbers. They also made the lead-lined gutters. Lead on the roofs only lasted about 150 years. Then it cracked and had to be replaced.

Cathedrals did not have drainpipes. Instead they had **gargoyles**. These were carved stone monsters, positioned just below the gutters. Rain-water drained into the gargoyles and spouted from their mouths, clear of the cathedral walls. The gargoyles were also there to guard the cathedral from evil spirits.

Workers employed at Westminster Abbey in 1253. White cutters were white-stone cutters or freestone masons – the most skilled masons. From 'The History of the King's Works'.

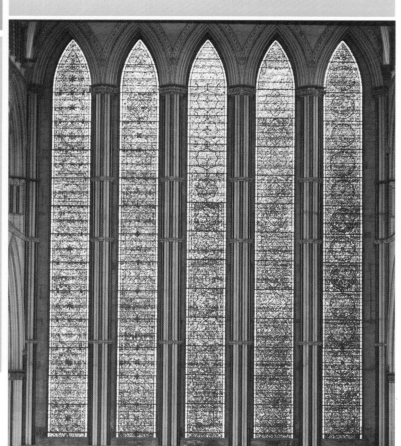

The Five Sisters window in York Minster which dates from 1260. This is grisaille glass.

The glaziers were needed once the window arches were ready. In the Middle Ages glass could only be made in small pieces – just the amount a glass blower could blow in a bubble, shape while hot into a cylinder and then open out. The pieces of glass were fitted together with lead between them. When they were in place the window was reinforced with iron bars. In Norman times, glass colours were dull greys and greens. This was called **grisaille** glass. However, by the 14th century glaziers had learnt to add chemicals to make brightly coloured glass.

It is believed that yellow glass was discovered in France when a substance picked up from the workbench on a workman's sleeve accidentally smeared on to painted glass that was about to be fired. When taken from the kiln this bit of glass was bright yellow. The substance on the workman's sleeve was chloride of silver.

From 'The Stained Glass of York', by A. C. Laishley, 1971.

The Great West window in York Minster made in about 1338.

Culmer

Richard Culmer was a preacher in Canterbury in the 17th century. We do not know when he was born or died. He went to Cambridge University. He then became a vicar in Kent. He was very much against decoration and ceremony in services. He was one of the ministers sent by Parliament in 1643 to demolish church decoration. He actually smashed stained glass windows himself. This made him so hated that he had to have an armed guard to protect him from the people. His extreme beliefs meant that one parish offered to pay him to go away and let them appoint another vicar.

4.7 Financing the Cathedral

Both cathedrals and castles were enormously expensive to build. Sometimes the land for a cathedral was given to the monastery or to the secular cathedral by a rich person. Sometimes the bishop built on his own land, as Richard Poore did at Salisbury. Landowners gave gifts of stone and wood. Pilgrims gave money at the shrines of saints buried in the cathedrals. Each cathedral or abbey had its own special saint – St Hugh at Lincoln, St Werburgh at Chester, St Thomas Becket at Canterbury and so on.

Another way for cathedrals to raise money was to sell **indulgences**. The Church taught that people could shorten their time of punishment in purgatory by confessing their sins to a priest (see pages 8–9). The priest usually told them to say a number of prayers so they spent time feeling sorry for what they had done. Indulgences were fines, which people paid instead of saying prayers. The money spent on indulgences went to the cathedral funds. The trouble with this system was that it became easy for people to believe that they could buy an indulgence and then commit as many sins as they liked.

For most cathedrals, however, the main sources of money were gifts from their own bishops, deans (at secular cathedrals) and wealthy local people.

One of the wealthiest people was the king. In the middle of the 13th century, Henry III wanted to rebuild Westminster Abbey. Henry set aside £2,000 a year for the work, but he could not always afford this. He often raised money by making people pay fines. The widowed Countess of Lincoln had to pay a fine of £4,000 for the right to keep her baby son after her husband died. The king told her to pay the money into the fund for Westminster Abbey.

A *Lanfranc, Archbishop of Canterbury, held 10 manors in Sussex. This is the entry in the Domesday Book for one of them.*

SOURCE

The Archbishop holds Patching himself; it was always for the monks' clothing. Before 1066 it answered for 12 hides; now 3 hides and 3 virgates. Land for 9 ploughs. 22 villagers with 21 smallholders have 6 ploughs. A church; woodland, 4 pigs .....

One hide was approximately enough land to keep one family, about 120 acres. A virgate was one quarter of a hide.

B William the Conqueror gave the Bishop of Winchester permission to cut trees in the Royal Forest for four days. The wily bishop gathered a huge army of axe men together and when the king found out how many trees had been felled he was horrified.

SOURCE

From 'Building the Medieval Cathedral' by P. Watson, 1976.

C

Task-works in 1286					
	Paid to	**Task**	**Rate**	**Payment**	
				£ s.	d.
10 Febr.	Richard of Longslow (Wlonkeslowe)	Making a smithy at the free quarry		12	2½
	Robert of Bedford	Making a scaffold		17	6
	Richard de Roden and Albert de Menz	Quarrying and dressing 1040 stones, each 2 ft. by 1½ ft. by 1 ft.	25s. per 100	25 10	0
	Richard de Roden and Albert de Menz	Quarrying and dressing 56 steps for the stairs of the towers	18d. per step	4 4	0
	Richard de Roden and Albert de Menz	Quarrying and dressing 200 ft. of string-course	2d. per foot	1 13	4
	Richard de Roden and Albert de Menz	Quarrying and dressing 40 ft. of voussoirs	2½d. per foot	8	4
	Richard de Roden and Albert de Menz	Quarrying and dressing 80 ft. of reveals of arrow-slits for the towers	5d. per foot	1 13	4
			Total for task-work:	£34 18	6½
		Sum total of expenditure on wages, carriage, purchases and task-work for the works of Harlech, 37 weeks 30 Dec. 1285 to 15 Sept. 1286:		£1602 18	6¼

Work at Harlech Castle in 1286. (Dressing stone – shaping it; string course – horizontal line of stone in a wall; voussoirs – stone blocks making an arch).

D

Expenses at Durham Cathedral 1422-23			
	£	s.	d.
Cloth from York	52	13	9
Wine from Newcastle	56	0	0
Horse shoeing and food	95	0	0
Repairs to buildings	60	0	0
Wages and pensions	100	0	0
Travelling and prior's expenses	45	9	11
Alms and gifts	15	14	11
Rent	25	0	0
Church taxation	23	0	0
Food for the year	790	0	0

12 d. = 1 shilling (1s.) = 5p
20s. = £1

Becket

Thomas Becket (1118?–70) was Archbishop of Canterbury from 1162–70, during the reign of Henry II. Though Henry and Thomas were great friends at first, they became enemies through quarrels about control of the Church. This led to Becket's murder in 1170. The Christian world was shocked at the murder. Becket's shrine became the most popular pilgrimage centre in England.

4.8 The Decorated Style

Exeter Cathedral is in the **Decorated** style. It is much more ornate than Salisbury. Walter Branscombe became bishop of Exeter in 1258. He had been to the newly built Salisbury Cathedral and must have been impressed by the lightness and elegance of the Early-English style. As soon as he came to Exeter, he started to rebuild the old Norman cathedral.

The building of Exeter went on for years. It could be that the great, great grandsons of the local labourers who carted stone for the cathedral were the men who saw it finished in 1369.

Exeter cathedral was like a rich greenhouse, compared with the plain, dark Norman buildings. Its windows were huge and every stone and wooden surface was carved with lush, curving lines of flowers, leaves, fruit and figures.

At this time wealthy people started to build chantry chapels inside cathedrals. They also left money in their wills to pay a priest (of the cathedral) to say prayers for them every day after they had died. These prayers were to shorten their time in purgatory.

From 'Piers Plowman' by William Langland, written in about 1370.

Langland

William Langland (1330?–1400?) is said to be the author of a long poem called *Piers Plowman*, which, among other things, criticized the way that the clergy lived. Little is known about his life. He may have been born in Worcestershire and attended a monastery school at Great Malvern.

From reading *Piers Plowman*, it is obvious the author knew a lot about medieval theology and the workings of the Church. He had obviously read a lot of books. He was quite prepared to be critical and to comment on the shortcomings of the lazy clergymen and monks of the time, who he showed as greedy and not really religious at all.

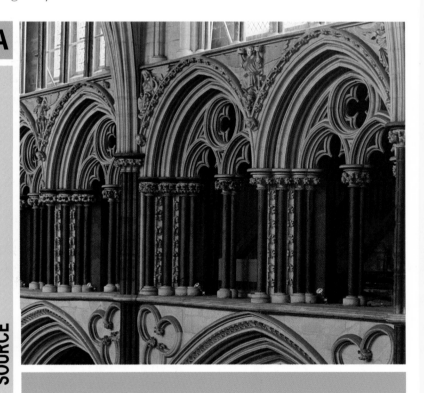

A SOURCE

The Angel Choir in Lincoln Cathedral which was started in 1256.

The east end of Exeter Cathedral. The canopy of the
bishop's throne is 18 metres high. It was finished in 1312.
Cathedrals are divided into three vertically. As you look
from the bottom to the top of the picture you can see three
clear levels. The large arches at the bottom are called the
arcade. The smaller arches above these are called the
triforium. The windows at the very top are the clerestory or
clear storey.

4.9 Pilgrimages

Saints were very holy women or men who lived good lives. Often they died for their faith in Jesus Christ. Saints were very important in the Middle Ages. People prayed to saints. Rather than ask God directly, a person asked his favourite saint to ask God for help. This help might be to cure an illness. Or it might be to beg forgiveness for doing something bad.

Often people travelled a long way to visit the **shrine** (tomb) of a famous saint. It was very important that a cathedral had the body or at least the **relics** (parts of a body) of one saint or more. The relics gave the cathedral great prestige. They also attracted **pilgrims** to pray, who gave money to the cathedral.

The most famous pilgrimage centre in Britain was the shrine of **St Thomas Becket** at Canterbury. There were other centres for pilgrimages – St Swithun was at Winchester, St Hugh at Lincoln, St Cuthbert at Durham, St Etheldreda at Ely and so on.

Etheldreda was a princess in Saxon times. After two marriages, she announced that she wished to become a nun. She retired to the island of Ely, which she owned. She built a monastery for both monks and nuns. They lived separately but shared the work. There were a number of monasteries like this in Saxon times and they were usually run by Abbesses. Etheldreda ruled over the monastery at Ely for seven years. Other women of rich and noble families joined her. People sent their children to be educated by her. She, herself, lived very simply. She wore coarse woollen clothes and ate only one meal a day. She had warm water for her bath only at Christmas, Easter and Whitsun.

Sixteen years after she died, her body was dug up to be put in a tomb in the cathedral. To the amazement of the monks and nuns the body had not rotted. This was the sure sign of a saint in those days. Immediately cures and miracles began to happen and the day was called St Etheldreda's day.

A

SOURCE

Remains of a 13th-century body. The crozier (curly headed stick) and mitre show he was a bishop. Bodies buried in stone coffins, in damp conditions and probably embalmed in some simple way, can sometimes be partly preserved.

Years later the monks of Ely were keen to have the relics of Etheldreda's sister, Withburga who was also a saint. The body of Withburga was in a tomb at Dereham Monastery. The king granted Dereham Monastery to Ely, but the abbot of Ely knew that Dereham would not give up St Withburga's body willingly. So he set off for Dereham with a party of armed men. They behaved as though they had just come to take possession of the lands. Everything went well. The abbot of Ely gave a feast for the people of Dereham.

Then, in the middle of the night, while the guests were sleeping off the effects of the feast, the abbot and his men stole the coffin and carried it 20 miles to the river where they had a boat waiting. They slipped the coffin into the boat and set off to Ely. In the morning the Dereham monks were furious. They set off in pursuit, but having no boat they had to give up. Ely had gained another saint.

Pilgrims praying at a shrine. Sometimes holes were put in the side of the tomb so that pilgrims could touch the bones of the saint. The monk is called a custos. He is guarding the tomb. The coiled 'snakes' are lengths of wax-covered string. People believed it was important to light candles to saints. The candles had to be the same length as the sick person, or sick part of a person. This was difficult if the sick person was tall. It was even more difficult if the person was praying for the safety of a ship at sea or a whole herd of cattle! In these cases they had to find the exact measurement, cut the string to the right length, coat it in wax and take it with them to the shrine. These lengths of waxed string were called trindles.

4.10 The Decline of Pilgrimages

Thomas Becket was a great friend of the King, Henry II. However, they quarrelled when Becket became Archbishop of Canterbury in 1162. Becket was murdered in Canterbury Cathedral on the king's orders. As soon as Becket was killed, the king was horrified. He went on a pilgrimage to Canterbury to seek forgiveness.

Almost immediately, miracles and cures were reported near the site of Becket's murder. He was **canonized** (declared a saint) by the Pope in 1174. From then on pilgrims flocked to his tomb.

This flood of pilgrims continued through the early 13th century. Then it tailed off a little until the jubilees (anniversaries) of his death in 1270 and 1320. After this, enthusiasm for pilgrimages faded so that by the 15th century far fewer people went on pilgrimages.

B

SOURCE

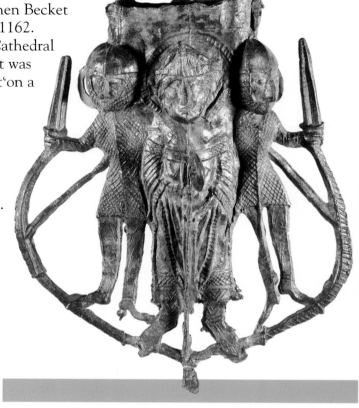

A pilgrim's badge. Canterbury Cathedral had two kinds of badges. One was an ordinary lead badge. The other had an ampulla or tiny flask which held drops of a saint's blood. Pilgrims bought badges at shops outside the cathedral. They wore them on their journey home. This showed that they had been on pilgrimages. The badge was also a souvenir and, importantly, anyone wearing a pilgrim's badge was supposed to be well treated by anyone they met during their journey.

A

Down to Canterbury they wend
To seek the holy blissful martyr, quick
To give his help to them when they were sick.
It happened in that season that one day
In Southwark, at The Tabard, as I lay
Ready to go on pilgrimage and start
For Canterbury, most devout at heart,
At night there came into that hostelry
Some nine and twenty in a company
Of sundry folk happening then to fall
In fellowship, and they were pilgrims all
That towards Canterbury meant to ride.

SOURCE

From 'The Canterbury Tales' by Geoffrey Chaucer, written in the late 14th century.

By the 15th century, trade was growing. More people had more money. This meant a growth in education for ordinary people, not just monks. There was a growth, too, in criticism of the Church. Pilgrims saw how much money was made at the shrines. This criticism became stronger as more people became educated.

C

SOURCE

Offerings at St Thomas Cantilupe's shrine at Hereford Cathedral on 29 August, 1307

170	silver ships
41	wax ships
129	silver images, either whole bodies or parts of human bodies (arms, legs, hands etc.)
436	whole images of people
1,200	wax images of parts of human bodies
77	figures of horses, animals, birds etc.

An uncountable number of eyes, teeth, breasts, ears etc. (presumably made of wax)

95	silk and linen children's clothes
108	walking sticks for cripples
3	carts
10	large square candles
38	cloths of silk and gold

many belts – men's and women's

many ladies' jewels including:

450	gold rings
70	silver rings
65	gold brooches and pins
31	silver brooches and pins

different precious stones

iron chains offered by prisoners

anchors of ships

swords, spears, lances and knives

uncountable number of candles

This list was made by commissioners from the Pope who were deciding whether to make Thomas Cantilupe a saint or not. The commissioners stayed for 78 days, during which time many more offerings came in. They do not seem to have counted the money offerings. Cantilupe's shrine at Hereford Cathedral did not attract anywhere near the numbers of people that Becket's shrine attracted.

D

SOURCE

Thomas Aquinas, lying on his deathbed, must have known that the men standing around him were thinking what a splendid relic he was about to become.

From 'Miracles and Pilgrims', by R. C. Finucane, 1977.

E

SOURCE

Henry went blind. His parents prayed and vowed a penny to Becket; no cure followed. They then went to Finchale, where he was healed at Godric's tomb, after which the coin intended for Becket was offered to Godric.

From 'Miracles and Pilgrims', by R. C. Finucane, 1977.

Cantilupe

Thomas Cantilupe (1218?–82) was educated in France. He became Chancellor of Oxford, then Chancellor of England in the Barons' War. When Simon de Montfort was defeated he went to France but then returned to become Bishop of Hereford and adviser to Edward I. Cantilupe was famous for his simple life. After he was buried in Hereford Cathedral, many miracles were reported there. He was made a saint in 1320.

5.1 Gunpowder and Castles

Gunpowder was one of the reasons why the age of the castle came to an end. But this did not happen quickly. Gunpowder was first used before 1326 and castles still played a big part in the Civil Wars between 1642 and 1653.

Both attackers and defenders could use gunpowder weapons. At first they were of more use to defenders. 14th-century guns were usually fairly small, but they were also very heavy and hard to move around. The first castle planned with the use of guns in mind was Queenborough, built between 1361 and 1375. It had two 'great guns' and nine smaller ones. Nothing of the castle survives, so we cannot tell how the guns were used.

There are surviving examples of **gunports** (firing places for handguns), from the 1370s and 1380s. They were near the castle entrances, where the fighting was expected to be fiercest. The noise and flame made by firing one of these early guns probably had as much effect as any bullets it fired.

It was much harder to use larger guns and cannon, than handguns, in castles. When fired, a cannon recoils backwards. Often, there was not space to do this on the thin medieval castle walls. If the cannon was fixed to the wall, so that it could not recoil, there was still a problem. The energy that would have been used in the recoil vibrated through the wall. This could cause the wall to collapse. It was some time before attackers got a real advantage from gunpowder. This came with the development of large cannon which could be moved around the country. Cannon had two great advantages over the old stone-throwing engines. They fired with a flatter **trajectory**, so they were easier to aim. Also they fired with more force, doing more damage to what they hit.

A

SOURCE

The Westgate, Canterbury, built 1380-81.

Gunloops

As with arrow slits, the problem with gunloops was to balance giving a good firing position against the dangers of the enemy being able to shoot through the hole.

In this type of gunloop there was very little danger of the enemy firing in. But the person firing the gun would have had no view to aim from. Gunloops like this were often built next to entrances because, if the entrance was being attacked, there would be no real need to aim.

This type became the most common. A small round hole to fire through (called an **oilet**), with a slit above to give the gunner a view of the target.

A siege, from a 15th-century manuscript.

In 1405, Henry IV captured three powerful castles, Berwick, Alnwick and Warkworth using siege cannon. Alnwick surrendered after only seven shots. The next year, he captured one of Edward I's great Welsh castles, Harlech, again using cannon. It was clear things had changed by the middle of the century, when the French captured 60 castles in one year from the English, using siege cannon. The balance of power was now clearly with the attackers, not the defenders. The high stone walls of even the strongest medieval castles could be smashed by cannon fire.

Simon of Sudbury

Simon of Sudbury (died 1381) was the Archbishop of Canterbury from 1375 until his death. He rebuilt Canterbury's Westgate with key-hole gunloops – state of the art technology in 1381. Sudbury studied at the University of Paris, then went to Rome as the Pope's chaplain. He came back to England as a diplomat, sent by the Pope to Edward III in 1356. He stayed, and continued to go on diplomatic missions for the kings of England.

Disastrously, his career moved into domestic politics. He became Chancellor and got Parliament to pass the hated Poll Tax in 1380. This was one of the main causes of the Peasants' Revolt. Sudbury sheltered in the Tower of London, but he was dragged out and executed by the peasants. As often happened, it was not a quick death – it took eight blows with the axe to cut off his head.

New castles were built even after cannon were effective. These castles, often called **courtyard castles**, were built between 1370 and 1480. They have a number of features in common.

- They were smaller than the great castles built in the previous 100 years.
- They were often built around a courtyard.
- The outside wall of the living space was also the outside wall of the castle, and therefore the main defence.
- The living space was usually much better than in earlier castles. If there was a conflict between comfort and safety, comfort was likely to be chosen.
- Many fewer soldiers were needed to defend the castles.

The three castles in this Unit include an unusually small example (Nunney) and an unusually large one (Raglan).

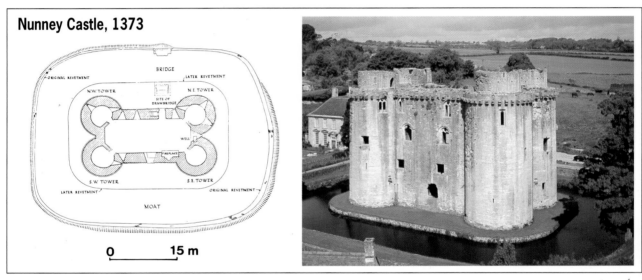

Nunney Castle, 1373

Bolton Castle, 1379

Raglan Castle, 1430s

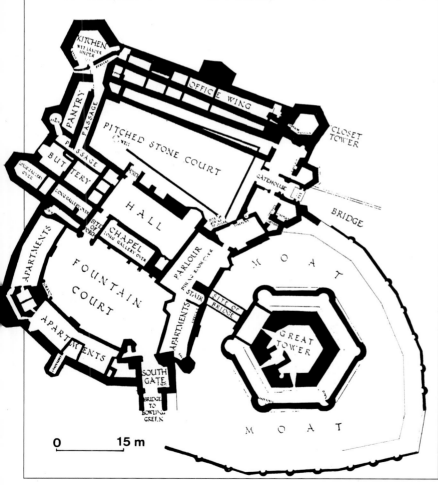

KITCHEN
WET LARDER
UNDER

OFFICE WING

PANTRY PASSAGE

CLOSET TOWER

PITCHED STONE COURT

GATEHOUSE

BUTTERY

LONG GALLERY OVER

PASSAGE

BRIDGE

LONG GALLERY OVER

HALL

SITE OF TOWER

CHAPEL

LONG GALLERY OVER

PARLOUR

APARTMENTS

MOAT

FOUNTAIN COURT

STAIR

SITE OF BRIDGE

APARTMENTS

GREAT TOWER

APARTMENTS

SOUTH GATE

BRIDGE TO BOWLING GREEN

MOAT

0   15 m

MOAT

Scrope

Richard le Scrope (1327?–1403) fought for Edward III in Scotland and France for nearly 40 years. He started work on Bolton Castle in 1379, and spent much time supervising the building works. However, he also became involved in politics, becoming Chancellor of England in 1378. Later he became entangled in the complicated politics of the time, siding against King Richard II between 1386 and 1389, and he spent many of his remaining years trying to aviod execution for treason. In 1397 he had to beg a pardon from Richard for his activities in 1386–89. In 1399 he was begging a pardon from another king, this time Henry IV. The castle was finished in 1397, but Scrope never lived in it. He died a natural death.

5.2 The Reformation

By 1500, the Church was wealthy. It owned perhaps as much as a quarter of all the land in England. The land was owned by the monasteries and cathedrals. The income of the Bishop of Durham was greater than any lord in England.

Some churchmen were not only rich, they showed off their wealth as well. Cardinal Wolsey built the huge palace at Hampton Court for himself. When so many people were poor and were told that Jesus Christ had been poor, it was hard to see the Christian Church displaying so much wealth.

In addition, the Church charged ordinary people for all sorts of things. Even the poorest person had to pay before a body could be buried in **consecrated ground** (land that had been blessed). They had to pay the Church to inherit from a will. They also had to pay **tithes** – a tenth of all they earned – to the local priest. This was to support the priest and keep the church in good repair. Some of these priests were no better educated than the villagers. By 1500, people were beginning to resent this.

On top of everything else, the Church had its own courts. They were separate from the ordinary law courts. They dealt with anything to do with religion. This included everything to do with marriage, death, wills, misbehaviour, heresy (not believing what the Church said) and so on. The fines and costs were high. The court worked slowly and was often accused of taking bribes. Perhaps the most hated church person was the **summoner** who travelled around the country summoning people to appear in the Church court.

These criticisms of the Church got mixed up with other events in the 1520s. Henry VIII wanted a divorce and the Pope would not allow it. In Germany, Martin Luther was challenging many of the ideas of the Church, especially the power of the Pope. All these things led to the **Reformation**. Between 1533 and 1536 Parliament made England a **Protestant** country with Henry VIII as the head of the church instead of the Pope. The monasteries were closed and much of the wealth of the Church was confiscated.

A

SOURCE

Wolsey

Thomas Wolsey (1475?–1530) was probably the son of a butcher. He went to Oxford and, when he was about 23 years old, became a priest. In 1507 he entered the king's service as Henry VII's personal priest or chaplain. When Henry VIII became king in 1509, Wolsey remained in favour. He became Archbishop of York in 1514 and was made a cardinal in 1515. He became very rich and built himself a grand palace called Hampton Court. His rise to power made him many enemies. Wolsey advised the king in foreign affairs. He had many successes, but he lost favour when he could not get a divorce for Henry from Catherine of Aragon. He had to leave the court and retire to York.

Perpendicular

Perpendicular style architecture followed the
Decorated style. It was in many ways even
more splendid. It took its name from the way
in which the vertical lines in the windows
were cut by straight horizontal lines. The
vaulting of the roofs spread out into rich
patterns like fans. But by 1500, there was little
new building going on.

Kings College Chapel, Cambridge. One of the best examples
of the Perpendicular style's fan vaulting in Britain. Kings
College is one of the colleges of Cambridge University.

Wolsey's fall

Wolsey had made many enemies because he was
proud, ambitious and successful. He was also
ruthless. His enemies hounded him once he fell
from favour. He was accused of treason in 1530.
He began the long journey from York to London
where he was going to be made to stand trial. He
would almost certainly have been found guilty and
executed. However, he became more and more ill
on the journey and died at Leicester Abbey.
Shortly before his death he said:

> I see the matter against me and how it
> is framed, but if I had served God as
> diligently as I have the king, He would not
> have given me over in my grey hairs.

The East Window of York Minster, made between
1405 and 1408.

5.3 Castles after Cannon

Through the Middle Ages castle walls had got higher. After all, this made them harder to get over. It also made them a much better target for cannon. Castle designers took a long time to work out good defences against cannon. The answer was to have very short walls, so that there was much less of a target to aim at. Of course a short wall would be easy to climb. To overcome this, there would be a deep dry moat in front of the wall. This meant the wall was higher than it seemed.

The Middle Ages had also seen a movement from earth banks, in motte and bailey castles, to stone walls. During the 16th century, designers went back to earth. Earth walls, often with an outer layer of stone, were much stronger against cannon fire. They just absorbed the force of the cannon shot, and did not shatter and collapse like stone walls. The final change was that walls got much thicker. For example, Carisbrooke Castle has a medieval curtain wall just over 2 metres thick, but the walls built in the 1580s against cannon fire are over 10 metres thick.

Short, thick, earth-filled walls were the solution to the threat of cannon. In spite of this very few castles were updated with this type of defence. Alongside changes in technology there had been changes in society. The castle, which had been both a great house and a fortress, no longer fitted in. Peace and law and order became normal, and the rich and powerful wanted to live in comfortable houses and palaces, not fortresses.

The last period of castle building in England was during the 1530s (see pages 60-1). Henry VIII built a series of castles along the south and east coasts. The idea was that these castles had large cannon which could sink the ships of any invasion fleet before troops were landed. These castles were built while the new ideas about defences were being worked out. They were still built of stone, but, 50 years later when Carisbrooke was strengthened, all of the new ideas were used. Also, during this time, a better system of flanking fire was developed.

Deal Castle.

BASEMENT PLAN
■ C.1540

0   15 m

GROUND FLOOR PLAN
■ C.1540
▦ LATER

0   15 m

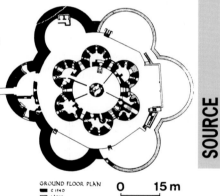

A cross-section through Deal Castle, showing the positions of the guns.

Dry moat   Dry moat

*An attacker's-eye-view of the new
walls at Carisbrooke. The photos were
taken from the numbered points
marked on the plan.*

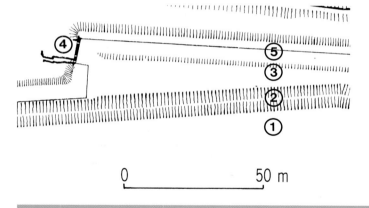

0   50 m

SOURCE

B

*Carisbrooke Castle from the air, showing the new walls of
the 1580s.*

SOURCE

Gianibelli

Federigo Gianibelli was an Italian engineer who
specialized in building fortifications. He worked in
Italy, but he also helped to design the fortifications
of Antwerp, and those of Carisbrooke Castle.
Italian engineers were the first to use arrow-
shaped defences called **bastions** (see Source C),
and were seen as the experts. Gianibelli came to
Berwick-on-Tweed in 1564 to advise Sir Richard
Lee about the town's fortifications after a wall had
fallen down. Lee ignored their advice and the walls
were never completed.